W9-CZH-835

The story of
the Bicycle

London's Ludgate Hill in 1886

The story of
the Bicycle

John Woodforde

UNIVERSE BOOKS
New York

119 2212

Published in the United States of
America in 1971 by Universe Books
381 Park Avenue South, New York,
N.Y. 10016
© John Woodforde 1970

Library of Congress Catalog Card
Number: 74-128402

ISBN-0-87663-135-9

Printed in Great Britain

Contents

London — comments in The Spectator *and other journals — velocipede mania in America — indoor rinks — first London-to-Brighton attempt abortive*

Illustrations

Acknowledgments

I would like to express my gratitude to Mr. Philip Sumner of the Science Museum, London, for reading most of the typescript and making valuable comments. I also thank for their help the staff of the Science Museum Library, the London Library, the Guildhall Library, *Punch* Library and Mrs. Evans of the Mary Evans Picture Library.

Sir Reginald Rootes and Mr. John R. Freeman have kindly lent me early documents and Mr. Douglas Weaver has taken great pains in photographing engravings. Mr. Derek Roberts of the Southern Veteran-Cycle Club has taught me—in conversation and through his writings in *The Boneshaker*—how to avoid at least some of the pitfalls of cycle history. Skilled re-spoking work by Mr. Reginald Luckhurst has made possible my own experience of riding a high bicycle.

Books made use of are named in the text and in the list of illustrations. I am grateful to the following for permission to quote short extracts from their books: Faber and Faber, *Over to Candleford* (Flora Thompson); William Heinemann, *Over the Bridge* (Richard Church); Geoffrey Bles, *Wheels within Wheels* (Geoffrey Williamson); the estate of H. G. Wells and J. M. Dent & Sons, *The Wheels of Chance* (H. G. Wells); Faber and Faber, *Period Piece*

(Gwen Raverat). In conclusion I must refer gratefully to the mass of technical facts in Mr. C. F. Caunter's *Cycles* (H.M.S.O.) which is on sale at the Science Museum.

J.W.

I

Empty Victorian Roads

Bicycles of a kind had been known for eighty years when the penny-farthing appeared in 1871. Yet this curious machine, with its front wheel between four and five feet tall, represented—and continued to represent for nearly twenty years—the most efficient bicycle the engineers could devise. The main factor in retarding development in bicycle design was the roughness of the roads.

The roads of 1870, eclipsed by railways, were actually worse than they had been at the beginning of the 19th century. An attraction of the spectacular tall bicycle, for those willing to mount it, was the way it coped with surfaces that were rough or waterlogged. The vast wheel, skilfully handled, both rode the bumps and held its rider well above the mud. And so ostentatious, moreover, was its manner of doing this, darting and swerving, that it seemed in itself a reproach to the surveyors of roads.

In the earlier part of the century the Turnpike Trust system, and the work of the engineers Telford and McAdam, had provided adequate highways for the long-distance coaches. But by 1850 the great coaching days were already over: the railway age had come. For the next thirty years or more the main roads were virtually empty of through traffic and received less and less attention.

Cyclists' protests about the winter quagmires they came across, the summer ruts and great lumps of stone, were countered by indignant retorts that 'ironmongery riders' paid no rates and consequently used the roads on sufferance. In the early 1880s there were still plenty of people who looked on bicycling as a passing craze. Flora Thompson recalls in *Over to Candleford* (1941) that

> cyclists in their tight knickerbocker suits and
> pill-box caps with the badge of their club in front
> were regarded as figures of fun. None of those in
> the hamlet who rushed out to their gates to see
> one pass, half hoping for and half fearing a spill,
> would have believed, if they had been told, that in
> a few years there would be at least one bicycle in
> every one of their houses, that the men would ride
> to work on them and the younger women, when their
> housework was done, would lightly mount 'the old
> bike' and pedal away to the market town to see the
> shops.

1   *Suggestion for Light Dragoons, 1874*

As things were, it was thought nothing to walk six or seven miles to buy a reel of cotton, or a packet of tea, or sixpenn'orth of pieces from the butcher to make a meat pudding for Sunday. Except for the carrier's cart which came only on certain days, said Flora Thompson, there was no other way of travelling.

Steadily the number of high-wheel bicyclists grew—in 1886 over 20,000 had joined the Cyclists' Touring Club—and some of them complained about the roads with a persistence unknown among horse-users. The Earl of Albemarle, who became president of the National Union of Cyclists, wrote in the 1887 edition of the Badminton Library *Cycling*:

> The only obstacle that I know of to the use of the cycle becoming universal in this country, is that year by year the roads seem in many parts of England to be getting worse and worse. . . . A revolt against the present system of road repair and surveying is being organised, and is likely to have a considerable success.

One of the first successes was a protest meeting of Birmingham bicyclists which led to eight road surveyors being summonsed for neglecting to keep their roads in proper repair.

The status of the bicyclist began to improve. In 1888 it rose abruptly when an Act of Parliament conceded that the bicycle was a carriage and therefore entitled to a place on the roads—provided a bell was fitted and rung continuously while the machine was in motion. In the end the bicycle came to be seen as the most powerful factor in reawakening the idea that roads were a national rather than just a local concern. Taxation returns show that between 1890 and 1902, a period in which bicycles rose in the social scale, the expenditure on the main roads of England and Wales increased by eighty-five per cent.

Countless lesser roads, however, were still, at the end of the century, in the care of small authorities—even parish authorities—employing amateur engineers. Their labourers had the primitive equipment of the 18th

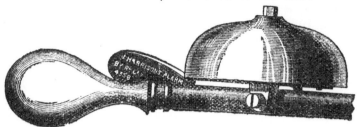
2 *Continuous alarm bell, 1880*

century: pick, shovel, basket and wooden rake. Scant notice was taken of a dictum of McAdam that no stone should be used for repairs that could not be put in a man's mouth. The repairers commonly threw down large and angular stones which left gaps for rainwater to fill up, and which, grinding on each other under cart wheels, rose unevenly to the surface.

Many local roads in 1900 were much as they had been in 1800. Country postmen, expected to cover twenty-five miles or more each day on a heavy tricycle, needed resolution and physical strength to get their machines across the stones and pot-holes. Typical rural roads of the late 1890s are described in R. E. Moreau's *The Departed Village* (1968)—a village in Oxfordshire:

> They were made of what is euphemistically called gravel, in effect flints dug out of the local parish pit by men who received tenpence for the cubic yard (measured in a box) and used their own shovels. The weight would have been about 17 cwt. The resultant

'gravel' was to some extent broken up . . . then
simply strewn on the roads . . . No roller was used,
and indeed the use of steam rollers on such roads
was well in the future.

An old man recalled in conversation with Mr. Moreau:
'Walking along on a dark night, the steel tips of your
boots struck sparks like it was a firework display'.
Ruts often reached a depth of six inches. The occasional
passing of a steam traction engine, or any vehicle with
wide wheels, was welcomed for its beating-down action.
In 1894 the Watlington coroner informed the highway
authority that he had been obliged to record this verdict
on a lady tricyclist: 'Accidentally killed by falling from
a tricycle in consequence of its coming in contact with
a large flint.'

3   *Sociable tricycle.* Punch *made the most of accidents. 1886*

Coroners rode bicycles now—or perhaps the staider tricycle. So did magistrates, chairmen of county councils and policemen.[1] As a result, highway authorities all over the country found themselves increasingly under criticism. But it was not till after about 1910, when the cars were appearing, that the great sealing operation with tar at last began in earnest. In a surprisingly short time the least of roads became a pleasure to bicycle along.

[1] As early as 1883 authority had been secured for the police inspector at Bournemouth to hire a tricycle 'which would be of great assistance to him and add considerably to the efficiency of the police in that district'. So it did, apparently, and a special shelter was built for it— according to Mr. M. Smith of the Southern Veteran-Cycle Club.

2

Hobby-horses

The earliest bicycles had no pedals or steering mechanism. They were simply beams on wheels, one behind the other, propelled by striking out with the feet as though skating. They could be made to deviate from a fixed direction only by lifting or dragging the front to one side; there was no need to acquire balance.

An 18th century Comte de Sivrac, a young man known for his eccentricities, is believed to have been the first owner—if not the inventor—of one of these crude machines. It took the form of a wooden horse fitted with two small wheels and was called a célerifère. In 1791 he showed it off in a Parisian park and the people there clapped and cheered, according to the researches of a French historian of transport[1]—especially the young women. De Sivrac seems to have worked hard for the applause: '*Il s'arrête de temps en temps, fort essoufflé, fort fripé, mais toujours souriant.*'

In 1793 the célerifère was renamed the vélocifère; and pushing oneself along on it became a pastime for some of the more dashing young men of Paris. A late 18th century print shows a group of *incroyables*, as they were called, riding in the gardens of the Palais-Royale. Races

[1] Baudry de Saunier, *Histoire de la Locomotion Terrestre*, Paris, 1936.

were run along the Champs Elysées. A comedy called *Les Vélocifères* was produced at the Vaudeville Theatre in 1804. But by then the initial enthusiasm was dying down: several participants had strained themselves in heaving at the machine to make it turn or were suffering from rupture of the groin.

In the year after Waterloo, Nicéphore Niepce, best known as the father of photography, produced an im-

4   *Célerifère, 1793*

proved vélocifère with a slimmer horizontal member and much larger wheels. The front wheel was still rigid, but demonstrations of the machine in the Luxembourg Gardens impressed spectators with its bustling speed.

The next year, 1817, locomotion on two wheels at last rose above a purely playful level: the German Baron von Drais de Sauerbrun succeeded in making a vélocifère with a steerable front wheel. He provided himself with a cushioned saddle, and a rest for the arms and chest to facilitate the work of thrusting at the ground with the feet. It is reported that when he first rode his invention in Karlsruhe, where he lived, the people fled in alarm and horses plunged about uncontrollably.

Von Drais was employed as a superintendent of forests and found the machine of use to him on journeys along forest paths. He once rode from Karlsruhe to Schwetz-

5 *Vélocifère, 1818*

ingen in an hour, along a route—mostly downhill—which on foot took over three hours.

In 1818 he brought the machine to Paris and called it the Draisienne. As a result of his performance in the Luxembourg Gardens, a new craze began. A draisienne rider covered the thirty-seven kilometres between Beaune and Dijon at an average speed of fifteen kilometres an hour.

France's amusing new sport was copied in England the same year (1818). Some draisiennes were advertised as swiftwalkers, though they were generally known as hobby- or dandy-horses. Denis Johnson, a London coachmaker who made various improvements, tried unsuccessfully to introduce the term pedestrian curricle. The novelty of the hobby-horse appealed to the Regency beaux, and hundreds were made and sold. Johnson turned

6   *Draisienne or hobby-horse, 1819*

out models for ladies with an ingenious dropped frame
to allow room for their dresses.

John Keats, the poet, said hobby-horses were 'the
nothing of the day', but *Ackerman's Repository of Arts
and Sciences*, in at least one article of 1819, spoke of their
possibilities for messengers, especially if travelling
pockets were fitted. The magazine also stated:

> For such as take exercise in parks, or have an
> opportunity of travelling on level roads, these
> machines are said to be beneficial. A person who has
> made himself tolerably well acquainted with one can,
> without difficulty, urge himself forward at the rate
> of eight, nine or even ten miles an hour. . . . And as
> schools are about to be opened to instruct young
> students in this country, we may expect to see
> them, ere long, brought into extensive use.

The riding schools apparently did good business. That
hobby-horses were played with extensively at this period

7   *Three views of the lady's hobby-horse, 1819*

is clear from a large number of prints by Leech, Alken, Cruikshank, Rowlandson and others. Most artists seemed to enjoy making the riders look absurd. The sport could certainly be laborious. Going downhill was a thrill, no doubt, but not easy or graceful in the absence of brakes or, on most models, anywhere to rest the feet. Michael Faraday, the great physicist, once attempted to ride a hobby-horse down Hampstead Hill. A safer and more popular venue was St. James's Park. Some riders were hampered by disbelieving that it was possible to maintain balance without help from the feet.

The new sport seems to have been vaguely irritating to the general public, perhaps because those who took part found they went best on footways, perhaps just because it looked silly; one often-repeated witticism was to the effect that hobby-horsers rode in their own carriages and walked in the mud at the same time. To those whose business lay with horses, it was downright annoying. A print of 1819 shows the blacksmiths of a posting village chasing a party of hobby-horse riders, upsetting them and smashing their machines to pieces with hammers. According to the caption, they were protesting over a threat to their livelihood: the hobby-horse, they pointed out, required no shoeing.

The great English hobby-horse mania lasted only a few years, killed as a fashionable pastime partly by the ridicule of the cartoonists and partly by the incidence of hernia brought on by the awkwardness of the rider's position and the jarring of the iron-clad wheels.

8   *Reluctant dealer in hobby-horses, 1819*

By the end of 1820 only a small body of enthusiasts continued to ride, though rarely in a public place. Such was the popular prejudice against the hobby-horse that for the next forty-five years little attention was paid to any invention which involved travel on two wheels. Few deserved it. In 1821 Lewis Gompertz of Surrey demonstrated a device whereby leg action on the ground was to be supplemented by use of the arms to drive the front wheel. The steering column of his hobby-horse had a toothed quadrant at the bottom which engaged with a

9 *Gompertz velocipede, 1821*

pinion on the front wheel hub; when pulled backwards, the handle turned the wheel.

It was with vehicles having more than two wheels that most inventors at this period hoped to realize visions of satisfactory man-operated transport. Several wondrous machines were assembled. Most of them made use of the principle of an axle bent into opposite cranks and turned by either hand or foot power.

The Aellopodes is an early example of a vehicle 'for accelerating travel without the aid of either horses or steam'. It was a kind of enormous tricycle, twelve feet long and with rear wheels six feet in diameter. The rider propelled it by stepping backwards on treadles connected with the axle. *The Mirror of Literature, Amusement, and Instruction* on 23 March 1839, gave the machine a splendid write-up, calling it 'light and elegant in form'. But it cannot be believed that the paper's correspondent had personally seen it going at the speed he claims for it. On common roads, he writes,

> this machine may be propelled at the rate of from twenty to thirty miles an hour; and we learn that many gentlemen of the University of Cambridge have adopted it as a means of exercise. . . . The inventor is Mr. Revis, of Cambridge, well-known as a talented mathematician, who has made offers to the heads of the post-office department, with a view to a speedier

14

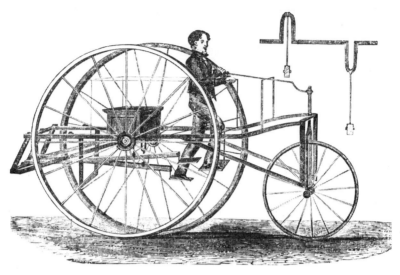

10 *Aellopodes, 1839*

11 *Consett tricycle, c. 1850*

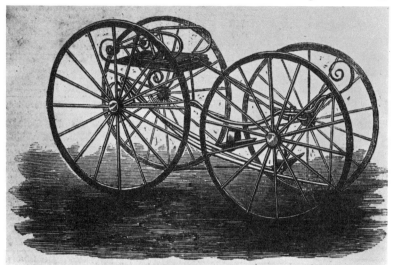

12   *Quadricycle presented to Prince of Wales in 1858*

and more economical transmission of the cross-mails. It is to be hoped that on the present occasion there will be less of that official delay which so frequently mars the true interests of the public when mechanical novelty is in question.

With four wheels, and upon rail-roads, the velocity would of course be augmented in a vast progressive ratio. Surmises having been thrown out with reference to the difficulty of moving up inclined planes, Mr. Revis has constructed a most ingenious piece of mechanism, wherein a lever, whether by elevation or depression, assures an onward progress without the possibility of the wheels *turning back*. Considered *per se*, the Aellopodes is a very striking effort of mechanical skill—simple and occupying little space.

From about 1845 the principle of propulsion by means of rods acting on a driving axle was applied experimentally to heavy three- and four-wheeled machines. The Science Museum, London, has a quadricycle made for the Prince Consort in about 1850 by J. Ward, a coach builder of Leicester Square. It resembles a child's pedal car blown up to something more than adult proportions.

Steering is by a single hand-lever connected with the fore-carriage. The frame is of solid iron but has a cushioned seat. The wheels are wooden with iron tyres, the driving ones forty inches in diameter. There are straps for holding the rider's feet to the treadles. The total weight is 115 lb.

Quadricycles of this sort were exhibited at the 1851 Exhibition and subsequently supplied to various crowned heads in Europe. They were admired for their novelty rather than because they were useful, except in a limited way. Makers rarely thought it necessary to fit a brake or a bracket for a lamp, so unattractive was the labour of progression on public roads. In 1849, Thomas Carlyle, the Victorian man of letters, rode a four-wheeled, treadle-operated, tandem 'velocipede' the twelve miles from Chelsea to Wimbledon and back (average speed, four miles an hour). His companion was an Italian portrait painter. 'Three hours,' wrote his wife Jane in a letter, 'that strange pair were toiling along the highways.'

Velocipedes

The first true bicycle, a two-wheeled velocipede that could be ridden with the feet entirely off the ground, appeared in 1839. In that year Kirkpatrick Macmillan, a Scottish blacksmith of Courthill, quietly finished work on a treadle-operated two-wheeler. It was a significant advance on the hobby-horse: the frame was a curved wooden backbone, forked to accommodate the rear-driving wheel and to carry the axle bearings near its end.

The machine aroused only local curiosity; though in due course various mechanically minded persons made copies and amused themselves with modifications. Macmillan's contribution to locomotion was not recognized till the last years of the 19th century when a plaque was attached to his forge with the inscription: 'He builded better than he knew.'

Macmillan's cranks were fitted to the rear axle and operated by means of connecting rods linked to wooden treadles which were suspended from the steering head. He often rode his machine the 14 miles from Courthill to Dumfries; and for short distances he made the wooden wheels with iron tyres grind along at 14 miles an hour. In 1842 he was fined five shillings at the Gorbals Police Court for knocking over a child in Glasgow at the conclusion of a 40-mile ride. Despite his performances, aston-

13   *Macmillan velocipede, the first rear-driven bicycle, 1839*

ishing at their time, there is no record of Macmillan having ever sold a bicycle.

Another twenty years were to pass before serious interest was aroused in two-wheelers. This was brought about by the coming of a seemingly obvious device, direct-acting pedals. The first machine with pedals was produced in 1863 in the workshop of Pierre Michaux, a Parisian coach repairer and maker of perambulators. His son Henry has left an account of how it happened— and of what is believed to be the origin of pedals.

In 1861, he writes, a customer brought in an old hobby-horse for repair. After a road test there was a discussion in the workshop about what to do with it. His father

14   *Needham tricycle, c. 1860*

then made the suggestion that a cranked axle should be
fitted to the hub of the front wheel, 'like the crank
handle of a grindstone, so that it could be turned by the
feet of the rider'. Henry's brother Ernest carried out the
suggestion. Today a national monument at Bar-le-Duc
recognizes that Pierre and Ernest Michaux were the
'inventeurs et propagateurs du velocipède à pédale'.

   The firm of Michaux soon began turning out pedalled
velocipedes on a commercial scale; by 1865, in new
premises, production reached 400 machines a year. The
wheels were nearly equal at this stage, about thirty-six
inches in diameter; the tyres were of iron and flat like a
wagon's. Although in general appearance they resembled

the despised hobby-horse, the novelty of pedalling brought good business—and a new excitement to the streets of Paris. *Harper's Weekly* said velocipeding there had become 'a fever', and that an active Frenchman could traverse ten miles of Paris streets in a single hour.

By 1867 pictures were appearing in English illustrated papers depicting young Parisians amusing themselves on pedalled velocipedes. The Rev. G. Herbert, a schoolmaster who became an official of the Cyclists' Touring Club, wrote in the 1890s an account of how the sport was first introduced to undergraduates at Cambridge. One evening in hall someone came out with the news that a dentist in the town had acquired one of these novel machines (soon to be known as boneshakers), and that he would come sharp round a corner on it and never fell and broke the brittle things he usually had in his pockets.

15 *Michaux velocipede, 1865*

Herbert lost no time in calling on the dentist, and through his agency bought a boneshaker. He had to learn to ride it alone, for 'the dentist's hours of liberty were not my spare hours'. It took him more than a fortnight before he dared venture beyond Tennis Court Road, the place he chose for practice because it was quiet and had a good surface.

He would prop the machine against a wall, cautiously climb up into the saddle and then push himself away. Day after day a wild plunge forward was halted by

16 *Michaux velocipedes being tried by the young Prince Imperial and his cousin while the Emperor Napoleon III (far left) watches, 1869*

either a charge into the wall on his left or by a spill in the dust on his right. To learn mounting and dismounting, he said, demanded application and a nimble frame:

> Grasping the handles, I set off at a fast run, keeping alongside the machine, till I got a considerable momentum on it, when I vaulted into the saddle. The spice of danger about it added to the zest with which I set about mastering it. After many bruises, sundry scratches and the expenditure of much unnecessary exertion, I at last mastered the art and was not a little proud of my accomplishment.

Several undergraduates wanted to follow Herbert's example; and the dentist in due course set up as a trader in boneshakers to supplement his dental earnings. But even with a smooth road to travel—and these were rare in the middle of the 19th century—the labour of bicycling in 1867 was formidable. 'A railway bridge', says Herbert, 'or some other slight rise in the ground, brought us to a standstill.' Overall weight and the rider's awkward position in relation to the pedals contributed most to the difficulties of riding these early bicycles. Soft roads, if level, were not necessarily a hindrance to the progress of wheels with flat tyres of iron; for as anyone knows who has tried it, the iron-shod velocipede will readily slip sideways on a perfectly smooth macadam surface.

But over in Paris, Michaux was working on weight reduction. At about this time he began making the front wheel markedly bigger than the back wheel. This allowed higher speeds, slightly reduced bumpiness and, of course, lessened the resemblance to hobby-horses. The first bicycle race was held at St. Cloud, Paris, on 31 May 1868, and was won by an Englishman, James Moore, then living in Paris.

In January 1869 one of Michaux's taller velocipedes arrived for demonstration at a gymnasium in London. It caused a sensation, for none of the spectators, apparently, realized that it was possible to remain upright on two wheels—that is, without putting a foot to the ground at brief intervals. This is how the event was written up at the time by John Mayall in the magazine *Ixion:*

In the early part of January, 1869, I was at Spencer's Gymnasium in Old Street, St. Luke's when a foreign-looking packing-case was brought in. . . . A slender young man, whom I soon came to know as Mr. Turner of Paris, followed the packing-case and superintended its opening; the gymnasium was cleared, Mr. Turner took off his coat, grasped the handles of the machine, and with a short run, to my intense surprise, vaulted on to it, and, putting his feet on the treadles, made the circuit of the room. We were some half-dozen spectators, and I shall never forget our astonishment at the sight of Mr. Turner whirling himself round the room, sitting on a bar above a pair of wheels in a line that ought, as we innocently supposed, to fall down immediately he jumped off the ground. Judge then of our surprise when, instead of stopping by tilting over on one foot, he slowly halted, and turning the front wheel diagonally, remained quite still, balancing on the two wheels.

The slender Mr. Turner was Rowley Turner, Paris agent of the Coventry Sewing Machine Company. In the autumn of 1868 he had brought over a French velocipede to show to his uncle, Josiah Turner, who managed the company. He rode it from Coventry station to the factory. His triumphant arrival there was later seen to be the start of the Coventry cycle industry; for he persuaded his uncle to produce 400 machines for the French market. By 25 February 1869, the firm had changed its name to the Coventry Machinists Company and was supplying the home market with velocipedes. Before long it was apparent that cycle manufacture was going to save the city from serious depression caused by a decline in the watchmaking, sewing machine and ribbon trades.

James Starley, known as the father of the cycle trade, was at that time a foreman with the Coventry Machinists Company. He had under him G. Singer and W. Hillman, both of whom became well known as car manufacturers. Starley contrived to improve the velocipede: wire spokes replaced wooden ones; solid rubber tyres replaced iron; a rear step was fitted for easier mounting.

Seeing the sporting possibilities, his company opened its own riding school and built a practice course. They advertised as follows:

> The Directors respectfully call the attention of velocipedists and the public generally, to the agreeable facilities they offer for gentlemen to acquire a thorough knowledge and perfect mastery of their celebrated bicycles. The grounds, which are strictly private and secluded, afford a most agreeable promenade for ladies.

In 1869 people who had not seen a bicycle in action were inclined to discount the stories of those who had. G. Lacy Hillier in the Badminton Library *Cycling*, 1887, writes of the experience of a friend who described at a dinner party a bicycle he had encountered in the City of

London. The gathering remained sceptical even when he
drew it. He was

> emphatically snubbed by a rude, if learned, philoso-
> pher, who clearly demonstrated to the entire
> satisfaction of everyone present the utter impossi-
> bility of the thing described being accomplished.
> The youth, naturally irritated at the doubt cast
> upon his assertions, or the accuracy of his powers
> of observation, sought for and eventually found a
> rider of the new machine. He rapidly learned to
> master it, and his first lengthy trip was a round of
> calls at the houses of the guests at the eventful
> dinner party, the learned philosopher being, of course,
> the first to be visited and favoured with a practical
> illustration of the fallacy of his theories.

Everyone who saw one agreed that the velocipede, or
bicycle as it was now being called, was a wonderful toy.
Hundreds were bought for their novelty value; and in
May 1869, only four months after the demonstration at
Spencer's gymnasium, *The Spectator* published a thought-
ful article about bicycle riding. It was not difficult, it
said, to understand the sudden popularity of the new
exercise:

> It is graceful, or rather there always seems to be in
> it the possibility of grace, while there is a certainty
> of attracting attention and fixing it on the per-
> former, which of itself would popularise any
> amusement with the French, and, perhaps, the
> English mind. Bicycle riding, like skating, combines
> the pleasure of personal display with the luxury of
> swift motion through the air. The pursuit admits,
> too, of ostentation, as the machine can be adorned
> with almost any degree of visible luxury; and
> differences of price, and, so to speak, of caste in the
> vehicle, can be made as apparent as in a carriage.
> It is not wonderful, therefore, that idle men sprang
> at the idea.

There was certainly room for a new vehicle, said the
article. Nothing was more wanted than a means of

Call it a toy indeed! Why, our ingenious friend,
Glimmer, has a run before breakfast, and grinds
his coffee and churns his butter with the greatest
ease. *Punch*, 1869

getting swiftly about on common roads without inces-
sant expense, for of all the drawbacks to country life
none had been more severely felt than the increase in
the cost of keeping a horse; but could the bicycle, if
unimproved, ever became a useful means of locomotion?

> The labour of forcing it along any ordinary rough
> road is calculated to be nearly equal to that of
> walking, but up an incline it is infinitely greater—
> greater, in fact, than if the traveller had to carry
> the velocipede.

The writer ended by suggesting that the velocipéde
might have to remain a toy used only by those who
liked violent exercise or who had 'a bitumen pavement
on which to display their address'. Other writers re-

minded riders and manufacturers of the fate of the
hobby-horse. *The Lancet* was inclined to be in favour of
the new exercise; but there were plenty of doctors ready
to warn the public that the machine had not been tested
long enough for it to be known whether it produced a
liability to injury.

The velocipede had got itself on the map in England,
it was a talking point, there were various enthusiastic performers; but there was not the wild fashionable
enthusiasm that had attended the coming of the hobby-
horse of fifty years earlier. In America, on the other
hand, velocipedes had become a rage. Two months before
the publication of the *Spectator* article, *The Gentleman's
Magazine* had this to say:

> The furor has migrated from France to our brethren
> across the Atlantic, passing over us. The go-ahead
> vehicle is exactly suited to American ideas. Schools,
> with the imposing name of Velocinasiums, for
> teaching the young how to gyrate, are being estab-
> lished; races are being rolled; men and boys are
> whizzing here, there and everywhere at a speed of
> twelve miles an hour. Inventors are improving the
> machines and are making them wholesale, the
> supply at present falling short of the demand. Our
> turn may come yet. Or have we had it?

Both *The Gentleman's Magazine* and *Harper's Weekly*
represented John Bull at that time as an amused spectator of Brother Jonathan's antics.

The craze captured New York in December 1868.
Harper's Weekly reported on 19 December the opening
of schools for 'the instruction of velocipede-riding':

> Youngsters ride down Fifth Avenue with their
> schoolbooks strapped in front of their velocipedes,
> and expert riders cause crowds of spectators to visit
> the public squares, which afford excellent tracks for
> the light wheels to move swiftly over. The Rev.
> Henry Ward Beecher has secured two of the American
> machines, and other gentlemen, well known in the
> literary and artistic world, are possessed of their
> magic circles. One of them takes his ride of nearly

VELOCIPEDES.

WOOD BROTHERS,
596 Broadway, New York,
Manufacturers of fine Pleasure Carriages, are now
prepared to receive orders for the celebrated
PARISIAN VELOCIPEDES,
of their own manufacture, which for durability and
beauty of finish are not equaled.

18 *American advertisement, 1869*

ten miles daily. . . . The winter season is not favourable to *veloce*-riding, but with the opening of spring
we may expect to see the two wheeled affairs gliding
gracefully about the streets and whizzing swiftly
through the smooth roads of Central Park.

Long before the spring the craze had spread to other
cities, and rinks were opened. The two best and largest
in the United States were to be found at Harvard Square,
Cambridge, according to J. T. Goddard's little book,
The Velocipede, published by Simpkin early in 1869. Harvard students crowded these rinks; the billiard halls
and other places of resort were deserted. One rink had
12,000 square feet of floor-space and twenty-five machines. The other, built in the form of an amphitheatre,
had a circular course of about an eighth of a mile. At
night, said Goddard,

this rink is brilliantly lighted, and the scene is at
once novel and inspiring. Scores of riders rush madly

after each other at break-neck speed, round and round the arena. We have seen an expert wheel over the course in 17 seconds.

The velocipede reached New Haven, home of Yale University, in the first days of February. On 21 February the *Yale Courant* published an article called 'Velocipedomania':

Every student and every other man seems to have velocipede on the brain. Two halls have been opened in the city for beginners, without meeting the great demand; and Hoad [a dealer] promises that a third shall be in readiness for the knights of the bicycle by Thursday evening.

On 1 March the *Yale Literary Magazine* reported that the usual charge at the rinks was a cent a minute, though Hoad supplied machines for out-door use at a half-dollar an hour. The thirty or more velocipedes at the service of the public were constantly in use and earning a neat little sum for their owners. Very soon, the velocipede emerged from the sawdust-sprinkled hall to flaunt itself on the sidewalks. Karl Kron, then a student at Yale, describes in his book *Ten Thousand Miles on a Bicycle*, 1887, how the allure of the new machine affected him:

No amount of absorption in books could deaden my ears to the bewitching rattle made by the approaching iron tyres upon the bricks; and when I gazed from my study window and actually *saw* an acquaintance proudly prancing by on a velocipede, my heart was quite gone. The charming spectacle enraptured my soul, and at the same time embittered it. I felt that I, too, must be a rider, or die! This sensation stands unique in my experience, and I can recall it as freshly as if it had happened to me yesterday.

Even today a normally athletic person learning to ride a bicycle for the first time when grown up would find it exasperating work. It was considerably harder to learn to ride one of the heavy, clumsy, front-wheel-drive velocipedes of 1869: a skill unthought of by users of 20th century bicycles involves continually adjusting one's hold on the handle bar against the tendency of each thrust on the pedals to change the direction of the front wheel. Kron had no more success at first than Herbert at Cambridge. He quotes from his diary for February 1869:

Saturday—I run one of the machines for an hour, without learning anything at all. Horribly hot work. Cool off in time for supper, and at 10 p.m. take another half-hour on the veloc. with no better result than before. Sunday—When the chapel bell summons me to put on my clothes, I discover that the seat of my trousers has been completely torn out. Monday— Instead of usual evening exercise at the gym., I chase up the veloc. for an hour, and learn how just a little. Tuesday—I rush right down to the velocipede hall, after morning recitation, and ride there for an hour. Eureka! I'm really a velocipedist at last!

On the Wednesday he indulged in two rides, and engaged a Pickering Velocipede for an early morning sidewalk spin on the next day. It snowed heavily, however, and he trundled the machine to the gymnasium and circled there for an hour. He repeated the experience next day. On the Saturday he had his first out-door riding and bowled along the concrete walks of a green.

Shortly afterwards a misfortune befell him by which he attained national notoriety. The facts, he says, were these: he was driving a velocipede slowly southward along the west sidewalk of Dwight Street on the afternoon of 24 February, when he noticed an old white horse, hitched beside the road, showing symptoms of fright. He dismounted at once. But though the animal was about fourteen yards away, it continued to be actively frightened. It writhed about, made a vain attempt at impalement on the hitching post and then threw itself down. However, it was soon brought to its feet again by some men who ran out of an adjacent carpenter's shop and appeared to have no injuries. The owner came up.

19   *Buell sprung velocipede (American), 1869*

Kron expressed his regrets and offered a payment to cover the probable cost of repairing a wheel of the cart to which the horse was attached: two spokes had been broken in the horse's attempt to kick itself free. The man accepted a dollar with apparent satisfaction.

The next morning Kron was hailed by an acquaintance with the news that the police had been visiting all the velocipede rinks to arrest the student who had scared a horse; and on returning to his lodgings at noon he found that official enquiry had actually been made for him there.

He went straight to the police headquarters and was told by the chief that there was no intention to arrest him but that, as a favour to the owner of the horse, a broker and general agent called Rosenbluth, he had instructed some of his men to find out the identity of the velocipedist. Kron went away to find Rosenbluth and ask what might be wanted. The latter said a large swelling had appeared on the spot where the horse had nearly run the post into his belly; he valued the horse at 150 dollars and would hold Kron responsible if it died, which seemed probable. All the same, he would accept a tender of 50 dollars in lieu of all prospective damages.

Kron did not jump at the offer. Instead he divided the sum of four dollars equally between a vet and a lawyer. The former, having examined the horse, expressed the opinion that its market price was not above 50 dollars, even without the swelling, and that this might soon disappear — as in fact it did. The lawyer advised him that he could not be responsible for any penalty. Kron sent a note to this effect to Rosenbluth, and was obliged to repeat its contents to him verbally when Rosenbluth came up and accosted him at a gymnasium. Kron recorded his final words at the interview in his diary: 'So you says you pay me nothing? Ver' well! I'll sue you, if it cost me five tousand dollar!'

He did not sue. What did happen was a report in the *New Haven Journal and Courier* of 26 February:

> On Wednesday, a student riding a velocipede, in attempting to cross a street in the upper part of the city, ran into a horse, throwing the animal down, and in attempting to rise the animal breached himself, and it is expected that he will have to be killed. The owner considered him worth 300 dollars, and calls upon the Junior for that amount. So much for the velocipede mania. We expect items of a similar character daily, soon.

The story appeared at the time when the boneshaker

furor was at its height all over the United States. It was just the sort of story all newspapers were eager to print, especially as it involved a young man at the famous Yale University; and before long there was hardly a city between Bangor and San Francisco whose paper did not give it a show. One paper boiled down the incident to a single line:

> A New Haven velocipedist ran over a horse and killed him.

In America the velocipede craze lasted barely five months. One municipal authority after another forbade riding on sidewalks. 'As for velocipedes,' said the *Yale Literary Magazine for* 22 May 1869:

> we can only tell, what we never expected to have to tell, of their dying days. Alas! Poor Yorick! A dire pronunciamento of the city fathers—'No person shall use or propel by riding thereon any velocipede along or upon any paved walk formed for the convenience of foot passengers, under penalty of 25 dollars'—has sent you to an untimely grave. Many disciples mourn their loss. . . . A couple of bold riders, who were arrested on the green, owed their release to the fact that *paved* walks were specified; but this quibble will no longer prevent strict justice from being meted out to all offenders. Anticipations of bright moonlight rides on the green, on summer evenings, have faded beneath the cruel blow. The best rinks with their best machines at 25 cents per hour cannot rescue the dying-out enthusiasm.

The prospect of having to try to ride on the uneven roads took away the attraction. But doubtless the ending of the craze had something to do also with its over-impetuous beginning.

In England, where there had been no such frenzied hopefulness, there was no sudden ending. While the American carriage makers dropped the velocipede in a hurry, and with a feeling of contempt for their own folly in having interrupted their proper business for such a

A NOVEL IDEA. TO BRIGHTON AND BACK IN NO TIME.

deceptive toy, English manufacturers had enough potential orders to justify a continued search for improvements.

The start of serious interest in the bicycle in England, as something that might be useful as well as amusing, came when the newspapers began to report records of long-distance rides. A machine that enabled a man to ride forty, fifty or even sixty miles in a day must, it was argued, be of some service.

The first attempt to ride from London to Brighton on a boneshaker was made in May 1869. The rider was John Mayall, who wrote the glowing account of Turner's demonstration at Spencer's gymnasium. He got no further than Redhill before becoming exhausted, and returned to London by train 'covered with dust and glory'. Shortly afterwards he made the attempt again, this time in the company of Turner himself and Charles Spencer, the gymnasium proprietor. The trio did the London to Brighton run in 16 hours, an achievement which was acclaimed by a *Times* headline as 'An Extraordinary Velocipede Feat'. But two months later their

21   *Phantom, 1868*

time was halved when C. A. Booth, a skating champion, rode his boneshaker over the same distance in seven and a half hours.

The firm of Michaux was very active in 1869. One of their 'improved velocipedes' brought the rider forward to enable him to make better use of his weight in pedalling. And it had wider handlebars to help in controlling the side-to-side movement of the front wheel.

At about the same time there appeared a British machine that was hinged down the middle. It had been patented in 1868 by W. F. Reynolds and J. A. Mays who believed they had found the answer to the various hazards met with in steering. The nature of these hazards are set out lucidly in their sales pamphlet which illuminates a half-way stage in the development of the bicycle:

> Almost the first thing the novice discovers on attempting to use the ordinary Bicycle, is, that the greater part of the power he exerts by means of his legs and feet, has to be resisted, or rather controlled, by a nearly corresponding expenditure of power on the part of his hands and arms. The front wheel is made to turn freely in the centre formed by the pivot

in which the steering fork holding the guiding handle
revolves, and it instantly responds to the lateral
pressure which is applied to it from the pedals, by
turning partly round upon its base: thus the moment
the right foot is applied to the pedal the wheel turns
round towards the rider's left shoulder, and *vice
versa* with the other foot.

While the Velocipede pursues a straight course, the
rider has only to control the lateral impulses of his
feet by means of the handle; but directly he puts the
Velocipede upon a curve, by allowing the front wheel
to gyrate towards the right or left, the observer will
notice that the front and back wheels are pursuing
different lines of motion; that, in fact, the back
wheel is more or less at right angles with the leading
wheel; and, as the whole of the propelling power is
attached to the front wheel, the effect is that the
hind wheel, instead of continuing its revolutions
exactly over the same course as the front wheel, as
upon a straight road, nearly ceases to revolve at all,
acts as a skid or break upon the progress of the
Velocipede, and makes a different course for itself
until a straight course is resumed. The effect of this
is, that, just at the moment when the rider requires
every possible facility for steering with dexterity and
despatch, as in turning a corner, or in avoiding
obstacles in the road, a drag is put on to the hind
wheel, and the manoeuvring must be accomplished
entirely by the strength and dexterity with which
he can, by means of the front wheel alone, resist
and overcome a skid or break equal to his own dead
weight. But here comes an additional difficulty. The
moment the front wheel is turned to anything like
a sharp angle to the line of motion, the rider finds
that the outside of the wheel is grazing against the
under side of one of his thighs, and that both his
legs are working at a disadvantage—one having to
reach over the outside of the wheel, and the other to
tuck itself under his body in a very awkward manner.
Those who are curious on the subject are recommended to pay a visit to a Velocipede School, and

note the fact, that while the velocipedists get along
gloriously upon a straight line, the moment they
attempt to turn, they are in imminent danger of
falling, and that novices do fall, and sometimes very
dangerously, in attempting to turn corners. If the
rider is resolute in retaining possession of the handle,
no matter how imminent may be his danger of falling,
the probability is that he will reach the ground com-
paratively unhurt; but if, as in nine cases out of ten
actually happens, the alarmed velocipedist relaxes
his grasp of the steering handle when going upon a
curve, the wheel instantly turns itself completely
round, and the rider comes to grief, but instead of
reaching the ground in comparative safety, his legs
will be blocked and entangled in a very painful
manner between the two wheels.

Reynolds and Mays turn at length to the way in
which their invention was to secure immunity from such
indignities:

The carriage instead of being an unyielding bar or
rod connecting the front and back wheels, is formed
of a framework made of steel bars . . . it is divided
into two parts in the centre, and jointed by a horizontal joint, so that the front and back halves move
or hinge freely to the right or left of the centre.
Steering gear is connected with the central joint, in
such a way that when the machine is moving upon a
curve, the sides of the front and back wheels are
made to approach each other as though one wheel
were about to be hinged or folded upon the other,
each turning upon its base as upon a pivot, and the
axles of each radiating or pointing towards the
centre of the curve or circle in which the Velocipede
is moving. The effect of this is, that, no matter how
sharp may be the circle in which the Velocipede is
moving, the back wheel is always pursuing the same
line of motion as the front one, and little or no
power has to be exerted upon the steering handle.
As the centre upon which the Velocipede turns is
independent of the wheels, it is impossible for the

ENGLISH MECHANIC

AND MIRROR OF SCIENCE

Engineering, Building, Inventions, Electricity, Photography, Chemistry, &c.

VOL. IX.—No. 222.   FRIDAY, JUNE 25, 1869.   [PRICE TWOPENCE.

22   *A suggested application for the velocipede. Note the ladies' side-saddle posture.*

rider's legs to come into the slightest contact with
the outside of the wheels; and, no matter what the
position of the machine may be—whether upon a
perfectly straight course, or turning a very sharp
curve—the rider's legs are always in a line parallel
to the course of the front wheel. It is thus impossible
for him to lose his treadles, and he is constantly
enabled to use the whole of his power.

The authors conclude by saying that the art of riding
the Phantom can be acquired with ease in a couple of
hours; that it can be carried upstairs or over difficult
ground as easily as an umbrella; and that it can be made
to go at twelve miles an hour. They contemplate 'an
extensive demand for such a Velocipede, combining as it
does every requirement of perfect ease, certainty and
safety of action'.

The experience of those who actually bought a Phantom was that the independent motion of the wheels
made it extremely difficult to steer. The effect, indeed,
was the reverse of what had been anticipated. The
Phantom never became popular but it eased the way for
a variety of developments. It made obsolete, for example,
the heavy wheel with solid spokes. The Phantom's
wheels represented the first practical use of the suspension principle (first patented by G. F. Bauer in 1802). Its
spoking consisted of lengths of wire threaded through
eyes in the rim and clamped to the hub with flanges; the
only omission, soon to be rectified, was a means of
tightening spokes which became untrue.

Tension wheels had, of course, a degree of resilience.
But their great advantage was lightness. Towards the
end of 1869 both the front and back wheels of boneshakers
were growing larger. The stage was set for the coming,
between 1870 and 1871, of the penny-farthing bicycle.

Penny-farthings

> How fast those new bicycles travelled and how
> dangerous they looked! Pedestrians backed almost
> into the hedges when they met one of them . . . it
> was thrilling to see a man hurtling through space
> on one high wheel with another tiny wheel wobbling
> helplessly behind.
> Flora Thompson, *Over to Candleford*, (Faber and Faber,
> 1941).

There were good reasons for the extraordinary shape of the high or penny-farthing bicycle.[1] The large driving wheel had a gearing up effect, while the smallness of the back one, a mere stabilizer, kept down the machine's weight. As well as being faster than any boneshaker— taller models could be ridden at over twenty miles an hour—the new bicycle was in several ways more interesting to ride.

The competent rider felt comfortable, even relaxed, sitting high up and upright astride his wheel. He liked the feel of the pedals almost immediately beneath him and of the short handlebar in his lap. He enjoyed the rolling billowy motion with which the high-wheeler covered the ground. Its progression was silent, too. There might be vibrations from the trailing wheel far below, but the single-backbone structure had no parts to rattle.

Did he look ridiculous? People often said so, but he himself knew that he was graceful and, in more senses than one, superior. He was able to reflect, while glimpsing the view over tall hedges and walls, that just to be riding such a bicycle meant that he had acquired a skill not

[1] The term penny-farthing dates from about 1890 when the high-wheeler, then known as the Ordinary, was obsolescent.

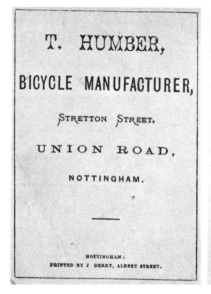

SPIDER BICYCLE.

Driving Wheel... ... ... 50 in.
Weight ... ... 40 lb.

23 *Cover and opening page of Thomas Humber's first catalogue, 1873*

within the reach of all. Few men over middle age attempted to mount and still fewer girls.

The most celebrated of the early high-wheelers was the Ariel, patented by James Starley and William Hillman in 1870 and put on the market the following year. It was the first all-metal bicycle that could be called light, and the first to have tension wheels (solid-rubber tyred) with spokes it was possible to tighten. The Grout Tension Bicycle, another famous machine, also appeared in 1871. W. H. J. Grout of Stoke Newington, London, was responsible for the weight-saving idea of making the front forks hollow and, in due course, for a variety of other improvements.

Within about two years the high-wheeler had turned the boneshaker into a mere learner's machine: in this role, however, boneshakers were invaluable, their comparative squatness allowing adult novices to learn the art of balancing without fear of falls from a considerable height.

The basic principle of the high-wheeler's design re-

A SUGGESTION FOR THE PARK.

mained unchanged throughout an ascendancy of about twenty years. Experiments and improvements were concerned with matters of detail. In 1874 James Starley patented tangentially arranged spokes, a method of spoking which is followed still. The rake of the front forks increased from two inches to between four and five. The short straight handlebar became longer and was then ousted for a type resembling cow horns which allowed the rider to straighten his arms.

While the front wheel steadily grew in diameter, the back one shrank. A writer to *Bicycle News* seriously advocated a six-inch trailing wheel, to be made of india rubber: the size eventually settled down at about seventeen inches. Brevity in this part was valued by some riders for the way it set off the grandeur of the front wheel.

The bigger the wheel, the higher rose a young man's self esteem. In the end, of course, he was limited by the length of his legs; and many young men aspired in vain to a sixty-inch machine. By the mid-1870s a usual size

25   *Ariel, 1870*

was about fifty-four inches.

At this date, so it can be guessed from contemporary estimates, there were about 50,000 high-wheelers on the roads of England. At least thirty firms were making them. The main centres of manufacture were Coventry, Nottingham, Wolverhampton, Sheffield, Birmingham, London, Brighton and Cheltenham. The *Daily Telegraph* commented on 7 September 1877:

> Bicycling is a healthy and manly pursuit with
> much to recommend it, and, unlike other foolish
> crazes, it has not died out.

By then 'bicycling' meant riding a high bicycle; it was the only kind being made. To nineteenth-century audiences at *Iolanthe*, it was the Lord Chancellor's elevated and draughty position that came first to mind as they hard him sing of bicycling across Salisbury Plain wearing only his shirt and socks.

NORTH LONDON BICYCLE SCHOOL DEPOT
AND AUCTION MART,
9, BRECKNOCK ROAD, CAMDEN ROAD, LONDON, N.

Instruction given in
Bicycling from 8 a.m. to
10 p.m.
Single Lesson, 1s. 6d.
Riding guaranteed,
10s. 6d.
Best floor in London.

Sales by Auction on the
first Thursday in
every month, at 8 p.m.
Terms—2s. 6d. entry,
and
5 per cent. Commission
on amount of sale.

AGENT FOR CARVER, TIMBERLAKE, PARR, AND OTHER
FIRST-CLASS MAKERS.

*Sargent's celebrated Bicycle Gloves, sent post free,
25 Stamps.*

C. WHEATON'S STANDARD BICYCLE for 1880.

35, LONG ACRE, LONDON.

CHEAPEST GOOD ROADSTER, 4s. per inch. of Driving Wheel.

CASH DISCOUNT OR HIRE SYSTEM.

WHEATON'S MAP of the BRITISH ISLES for Bicycle Tourists. Hills, Roads,
Railways, and smallest Villages. One Sheet, 50 inches by 40 inches, coloured,
30 stamps, post-free.

WHEATON'S WATERPROOF SADDLE POUCH. No straps required, 14 stamps.
Solid Leather, with straps, 20 stamps.

BICYCLES LENT BY THE MONTH. Enclose Stamp.

26   *Typical advertisements of 1880*

27   *Dogs and children caused headers*

The prime drawback, cheerfully accepted by the agile, was that the high-wheeler was unstable. Though it rolled smoothly over lesser bumps and dips, an angular obstruction such as a brick could check its progress alarmingly. The whole thing tipped over. Too hasty application of the brake, normally a spoon type clamping down on top of the front tyre, could easily cause the same result.

Falling forwards was a mishap that happened even to experienced riders. 'The manoeuvre is so common', wrote the Earl of Albemarle in 1886, 'that the peculiar form of tumble that ensues is known by the distinctive name of "the cropper" or "Imperial crowner".'[1]

Dogs, pigs, chickens and children often brought about these accidents. So did quite small objects suddenly encountered. Lord Albemarle writes that his son, Arnold Keppel, was going at his best pace once through a line of spectators when he ran over a piece of coal dropped from a cart. The bicycle turned so complete a somersault that Keppel came uppermost again. However, he was 'unconscious of anything from the moment his head and shoulders touched the earth until he found himself in a cottage being brought to with restoratives'.

In most cases these headers could be taken in such a way that barely a scratch resulted. Karl Kron, an American marathon bicyclist, has recorded numerous falls in *Ten Thousand Miles on a Bicycle;* none of them involved injury to his head or face. But there were occasions when he was embarrassed by plunging forwards while riding quite slowly. In 1885 he was setting off on a thousand mile tour of North America when

the very first thing that happened to me after mounting my wheel at the door of the Michigan Exchange Hotel, at Detroit, in the presence of certain cyclers who wished me good luck for my Canadian journey, was a violent header at a hole in the wooden pavement a few rods distant. Though I had steered clear of this same hole when I came in an hour before, I

[1] He contributed to G. Lacy Hillier's *Cycling*, in the Badminton Library of Sport.

forgot about it in the glare of the gas light; but I rode to the ferry without further accident. . . .

He reports that on the second day, 102 miles from the start, he took another 'bad header, without apparent reason, while slowly descending a rough clay hill'.

Another cause of falls was getting a foot amongst some part of the great expanse of spoking. Contemporary manuals urged caution when the rider was dismounting and feeling for the step. Occasionally, but only occasionally, the falls had serious consequences; riders lost control down hilly roads that took a sharp bend at the bottom, or fell over parapets into deep water. Reports of cycling calamities are not uncommon in the files of newspapers. The following is an example:

> Fatal Bicycle Accident.—Yesterday morning Mr. W. Carter held an inquest at St. Thomas's Hospital on the body of John William Runnegar, aged 26, a schoolmaster. . . . On the morning of the 18th inst, he was proceeding along Oil Mill-lane, Kingston [Surrey], on a bicycle, when, in attempting to get out of the way of a boy walking through the lane, the machine swerved, and his foot got entangled in the wheel, causing him to pitch headforemost into a ditch by the roadside. In his descent his right eye came in contact with the branch of a tree. *The Times*, 24 May 1884

Falls were so much an accepted part of bicycling that manufacturers made a selling point of their machines' ability to withstand them. Thomas Humber in his first *Humber Bicycle Catalogue*, issued in 1873, prints among others these alarming testimonials for his English Spider:

> Dear Sir,—I am very pleased, in compliance with your desire, to give my opinion of the bicycle you made for me . . . having had it several months in constant requisition, it is quite as firm as when I had it, notwithstanding a tremendous shaking and concussion it experienced on the occasion of a spill last September, after which I quite expected to see

it fall into fifty pieces. . . .

Dear Sir,—I purchased one of your Spider Bicycles some two years ago, and although it has been ridden on an average about 60 miles per week, and on several occasions been engaged in universal spills and collisions, it is now almost as sound as when first despatched from your works. . . .

The first buyers were young men of means and nerve; they might be professional men, clerks, schoolmasters or dons. Leonard Huxley (son of T. H.) crossed the Simplon on a high-wheel bicycle. The late Sir Sidney Harmer, the scientist, often rode one between Cambridge and Norwich and, according to his daughter Lady Gaddum, he played the game of counting the number of times he was thrown off and of trying to reduce it on each journey.

28   *High-wheeling in France, 1880*

Hilaire Belloc rode a high-wheeler professionally in 1889. He was sent at nineteen as the *Pall Mall Gazette's* 'cycling correspondent in France' to find out what he could about public opinion in the French provinces. Various chain-drive bicycles were already on the market, but Belloc bought for his purpose a brand new penny-farthing (as they were just beginning to be called), choosing a Rapid made by the St. George's Engineering Company of Birmingham. He wrote in his first despatch

29 *Labourer, 1886*

that it beat any other bicycle of the tall kind that he had ridden:

> . . . whether this is because of the larger hind wheel, of the saddle adjustment, or of the tangential spokes, I do not know; but certainly no other machine with which I am acquainted gets one to the top so easily and runs so smoothly.

The prosperous Victorian businessman, saying morning prayers with his household before breakfast, did not have a high-wheel bicycle: his cycling days began, if ever, with the coming of the tricycle around 1880.

Because a new machine cost £12 or so, the equivalent of £70 today, the labourer who would have been thankful to pedal to work could not afford it until machines became available on the cheap second-hand market. Then, workmen treasured their purchases—costing a few shillings—and many were still riding them in defiance of fashion and risk after the year 1900. A middle-aged Cambridge gardener was using a high-wheeler as his normal transport as late as 1909; an Ashford, Kent, lamplighter was still riding his up to 1914, finding it helpful in his work.

The mainly young riders of the high-wheel bicycles were long referred to as cads on castors. Cads, because of the tendency to swerve about and frighten horses (the King of the Belgians was once reported to have been thrown from his horse by a bicyclist bumping into it); castors, because the hind wheel appeared to swivel.

Until at least the mid-1880s, bicyclists had to put up with derisive cheers and with being loudly informed that their wheel was going round. 'Monkey on a wire! monkey on a wire!' was a popular cry. Another was 'monkey on a gridiron!', according to the Rev. L. Meadows White, author of *A Photographic Tour on Wheels*. The witticisms inflicted no injury, he observed in an article,

> but when to words are added deeds, and stones are thrown, sticks thrust into the wheels, or caps hurled into the machinery, the picture has a different

aspect. All the above in certain districts are of common occurrence, and have all happened to me, especially when passing through a village just after school is closed. The playful children just let loose from school are generally at this time in an excitable state of mind.

It was found quite easy to engineer an amusing header by placing a row of bricks or a length of string across the path of an oncoming bicyclist. A stout rod poked with deliberation among the spokes would inflict enough damage to give an attacker plenty of time to get away.

There were several reasons for the outbreaks of antagonism. There was the astonishment, turning into vague irritation, of the benighted countryman of *Punch*, bolting from an apparition that looked like 'a man a-riding upon nawthin'; there was the tiresomeness of beholding a fast-moving person who looked at once ridiculous and solemnly pleased with himself. And a lot of people considered bicycles a danger to pedestrians and said they had no right to be on the roads where the horses went.

The law, as represented by the magistrates, often said this, too—in the days before bicycles became high fashion—just as it did later about the mud-splashing horseless carriages and the caddish people who drove them. Brushes with the law were common in London and many found their way to the police courts. The favourite offence, 'riding furiously', was often said to have taken place on some of the new streets that were smoothly paved with wood. Mounted patrols of policemen made numerous successful raids on the high road between Kensington and Hammersmith, which attracted bicyclists and tricyclists on account of the excellence of the wood paving.

To go by the police reports in the papers, even riders of the weighty tricycle of 1881 had no trouble in doing 14 miles an hour. Evidence that is clearly absurd would be given by policemen who had received no proper instruction, and certainly no stop watches, to help them calculate the pace of bodies in motion. In December 1881

30   'The sensation of nearly flying', 1886

31 *The bicyclist and the law, 1880*

Wheel World facetiously described a typical court hearing. Four men are charged with furiously riding bicycles:

> Police constable ZYX 4002 deposed that he was on duty the previous evening, and saw the defendants riding at a rate of forty miles an hour; he walked after them and overtook them . . . taking them to the station handcuffed.

No doubt people often did ride too fast in places where they should have been cautious. Certainly pedestrians got knocked over, partly because some riders of the high-wheeler found it impossible to keep a straight course and partly because pedestrians were unaccustomed to behaving with the road sense which motor traffic has now made almost instinctive.

The professional drivers of carriages and other horse-drawn vehicles had their own reasons for resenting the high-wheeler. It could overtake them even when they were going at full speed: it often did, too, the rider glancing exultantly over his shoulder.

From time to time there appeared newspaper reports of acts of interference against bicyclists by drivers. A particularly flagrant attack occurred on 26 August 1876, when the driver of the St. Albans coach lashed an over-taking bicyclist with his whip, while the guard actually threw an iron ball, which he had secured to the end of a rope, between the spokes of the big wheel. The driver was fined £2 with £10 damages; the guard was fined £10.

Sometimes the bicyclist overtaking a coach with a flashing of spokes had no kind of teasing intent, but was undertaking a speed test between two places—probably on behalf of the maker of his machine. All kinds of racing, on the roads and on special tracks, were becoming a feature of English life.

Racing materially affected the design of high-wheelers, just as twenty years later it was to affect the development of the motor car. Racing men demanded lighter and yet lighter machines. Thomas Humber of Nottingham was one of the first bicycle makers to realise that the existing bicycles were unnecessarily heavy. As a result of considerable labour, he produced a racing bicycle which was thought a marvel of lightness and strength. Thereafter the makers vied with each other to reduce weight.

Inevitably, some racers appeared which were so fragile that they lost their shape or otherwise broke down in use. But in the early 1880s machines weighing twenty-four pounds or less were being made with sufficient strength to carry men of twelve stone over the racing paths. Bicycles not specifically intended for racing became lighter, too. Heavy joints, clumsy tubes and unnecessary solids were eliminated.

While all these things were happening in England, the public of the United States seemed to have lost all interest in the bicycle after the abrupt ending of the American boneshaker craze. Commercial production of the high-wheeler did not begin until 1878. But it began with copies of the best English models and soon re-awakened a demand for bicycles.

In America, riding a high-wheeler seems to have attracted less jocularity from spectators than in England. A writer in *The Wheelman* of 1882 observed that this kind of bicycle, swift and noiseless, transformed the solitary traveller into

> a personage of consequence and attractiveness. He becomes at once a notable feature in the landscape, drawing to himself the admiring gaze of all whose eyes are there to see. . . . His presence illustrates a fresh triumph of mind over matter. All creatures

32 *Racing man, c. 1885*

who ever walked have wished that they might fly;
and here is a man who can hitch wings to his feet.

Karl Kron, author of *Ten Thousand Miles on a Bicycle*
was not bothered by members of the public shouting at
him and trying to put sticks between his spokes. Instead,
whenever he stopped, he would be surrounded by an
interested group, anxious to learn about his movements,
though unwilling to ask 'direct questions which might
be resented by such a distinguished traveller'. To make
sure that he looked distinguished, Kron wore on his
journeys a shirt and breeches of white flannel and a
jacket of glossy velveteen. He also brightened at regular
intervals the nickled spokes of his wheel. In ways like
these Kron sought to rise above the fact that he was
often spattered with mud or grazed from a fall.

The falls experienced by riders seem to have had a
worse effect on trade in America than in England; and
much thought was given, at an early stage in the new
bicycling era, to the matter of designing a machine that
was not subject to tipping forwards.

In 1881 the Smith Machine Company of New Jersey
produced an allegedly safer version of the high bicycle
called the Star. It had the large wheel behind and the
small one in front—in a manner of speaking, anyway—
and was said to make falling forwards impossible since
the rider's weight was above the back wheel. Although
nervous people were afraid of falling over backwards,
the Star sold well for several years. It was propelled by
levers with a strap and pawl and offered the peculiarity
that each treadle worked independently; indeed, for a
sudden spurt, both feet could be pressed down together.

Surprisingly, it was found that the Star travelled
quite well over rough ground. An English visitor from
Swansea—Stanley Heard—tried it out on a railway
track and reported that he rode several miles over the
sleepers.

But the Star was a heavy machine and to steer it
properly a skill which could only be acquired with much
practice. Some enthusiasts developed this skill to the
point of perfection. In 1886 the *Pittsburg Dispatch* reported 'a daring and foolhardy feat' by the rider of a

Star at Cabin John Bridge, twelve miles outside Washington. The bridge, it explained, consisted of a single 200 ft. arch which spanned a deep and rocky gorge; the place had become a pleasure resort and the inn at one end of the bridge a rendezvous for Sunday hikers and bicyclists. One Sunday afternoon

a lively party within could be heard telling stories and boasting of their personal skill on the road. In the midst of the hilarity one young man suddenly came out alone, and, singling out his machine, mounted, and without a word rode towards the bridge. There is a brownstone coping on the three-foot wall on either side of the roadway. This coping is about a foot broad, and is bevelled on the two upper edges for an inch or two. On the inside of these walls is the solid roadway above the duct. On the outside is a perpendicular descent of about 125 feet in the centre of the bridge, and no less than 75 feet

33 *American Star, 1881*

34 *Prowess on a Star*

at either abutment. The young man stopped and dismounted at the end of the bridge and lifted his
machine upon the coping. The act was noticed by a
couple of gentlemen smoking under the trees, but it
was looked upon as a freak, and no particular attention was paid to it.

The next moment there was an exclamation of
horror, for the young man was seen mounted upon
his bicycle deliberately riding along the narrow
coping. The sight froze the blood of the ladies and
children picnicking in the gorge below, and was
enough to appal the stoutest heart. The gentlemen
in front of the hotel started to their feet and called
to the other wheelmen within. It was too late. The
young man was already in the centre of the bridge.
He never swerved a hair's breadth from his seat.
From the end of the bridge he seemed a toy machine
running by mechanism, so erect and motionless he sat.

'Let him alone,' cried one of his companions, 'he
could ride it if it was a rope!' . . . the fear that
interference might hasten the horror that all wished
to prevent left the party rooted to the spot. In two
places the coping makes a zigzag by the widening of
the roadway, and at these places the rider must steer
his wheel through a very narrow space at nearly
right angles with his course. The daring fellow had
passed the first of these ticklish spots, and, when he
carefully wore round the second, not a single one of
the horrified spectators could draw a breath for fear.
From thence to the end was a short and straight run,
and in another moment the young man had completed his dangerous ride, dismounted, and was
waving his hand laughingly at the frightened men
and women and children who had witnessed it. He
calmly remounted his wheel and rode on towards
the city. . . .

The American Star was not seriously taken up in
England. But even while the high-wheeler was at the
height of its popularity (when scarcely any other sort of
bicycle was seen on the roads), great efforts were being

35 *Xtraordinary, 1878*

made behind the scenes to invent something safer and
not less fast: apart from falls, it was by no means simple
to stop as quickly as events often demanded in heavy
traffic.

The early attempts were all based on the high-wheeler.
The saddle was moved further back. But it was found
that this made pedalling harder, and that vibrations
from the small back wheel became uncomfortably
noticeable once it was taking a greater proportion
of the rider's weight. The back wheel was enlarged: this
made the bicycle heavier. Pedalling by indirect means
seemed the only way to seat the rider lower down and
further back. As the front wheel remained the driver,
some curious-looking machines resulted.

THE "FACILE" BICYCLE

(BEALE & STRAW'S PATENT)

Bicyclists! why risk your limbs and lives on high Machines when for road work a 40in cr 42in. "FACILE" gives all the advantages of the other, together with almost absolut safety. A person of average height may ride a "FACILE" of any size, from 36in. to 42in. The most nervous person may ride the smaller Machine, since the feet are close to the ground, while even with these any reasonable speed may be attained. The action of the feet is vertical, and this gives greater power than the other, as is shown by the ease with which bad hills are mounted. There is no fear of going over the handles, and the powerful Brake may be applied without danger. Intending Purchasers and others are invited to call and inspect the Machine, and wherever practicable, opportunities for Free Trial will be gladly afforded to those who are riders.
Descriptive Circular and Testimonials will be sent on application.

SOLE AGENTS:—

ELLIS & CO.,

(LATE OF 42, HART STREET, BLOOMSBURY,)

165, FLEET STREET, LONDON.

(Adjoining Anderton's Hotel.)

The most celebrated of the bicycles then known as safety ordinaries were the Xtraordinary of 1878, the Facile of 1879 and the Kangaroo of 1884. In the first two levers were used to bring the pedals nearer the ground; in the third, chains. The question of up-and-down versus rotary action was constantly debated at that time. H. W. Bartleet, in an article in *Cycling* (1942), writes that the lever action lent itself to the use of varying power, but the direction of force was changed so fast that some back pressure on the pedals was unavoidable: the rotary action was superior for speed.

All three of the safety ordinaries demonstrated a trend towards shrinking front wheels and expanding back ones. The Facile, patented by John Beale several years before it appeared on the market, had the front wheel reduced to forty-four inches.

The Kangaroo, patented by E. C. F. Otto and J. Wallis, was even more of a departure in that its front wheel was only thirty-six inches in diameter. But an arrangement of short chains and sprockets with a step-up ratio compensated for the decrease in diameter; in fact the wheel was so geared that it could cover for each revolution of the pedals the same distance as a fifty-four inch wheel. On 27 September 1884 G. Smith covered a hundred miles

37   *Facile rider in the tight-fitting uniform of the Facile Bicycle Club (headquarters: The Green Man, Blackheath), 1883*

38   *Kangaroo, 1885*

on a Kangaroo in seven hours seven minutes—then the fastest time on record for any cycle.

The makers, Hillman, Herbert and Cooper of Coventry, advertised their product so energetically that the public was persuaded that despite their diminutive size, the Kangaroos deserved notice. They were especially recommended for 'heavy, steady or nervous road riders'. The machine was constructed throughout, said the publicists, with an eye to satisfactory road work, and thus

the gearing is a matter of individual taste when ordering; some Safety riders have two sets of bottom pulleys, and alter to a lower gearing for winter riding. . . . The handles are conveniently placed, and

39 *William Hillman, W. H. Herbert and G. B. Cooper, who were responsible for the manufacture of the Kangaroo*

are bent downwards in cow-horn fashion, affording
a good straight pull up hill. . . . As the foot-rests are
practically part and parcel of the front forks, they
assist materially in controlling the steering, and
nothing is so exhilarating as a rush down-hill on a
Kangaroo, with feet on the foot-rests, the body
thrown well back, the arms straight.

The 1887 edition of *Cycling* set out three points which
a man coasting on a Kangaroo should attend to:

1. To get his feet well up on the foot-rests: if the
point of the foot only is allowed to rest on it, there
is the very possible chance of the heel catching the
pedal, which might cause a nasty fall.
2. As the foot-rests are carried so far in front of the
axle, to counterbalance the effect of the weight and
pressure there, the rider must be careful to throw
his body as far back as possible.

40   *Beeston Humber tandem, 1885*

3. The brake, which is a very powerful one, should be applied very gradually, as its sudden application would send the rider over the handle-bar.

The last two points were of course just those which inhibited some people from mounting the high-wheeler. The kangaroo-type of bicycle reduced risk only in that the rider had rather less far to fall.

e so-called safety was designed to take two people. Beeston Humber Tandem Safety of 1885 was in fact st tandem bicycle; the riders were carried, one the other, on top of the big wheel and—as with er tandem tricycle which inspired this machine wheel did the steering and was controlled by ider. This kind of tandem never became popu- Lacy Hillier wrote optimistically in 1886:

it will prove a practical success time alone but arguing from the results obtained on
i   ycles, it should prove very fast, and, as
a   me time obviously safe, there may be
it.

All   rties, of course, could be taken with
these   the high-wheeler by the young and
the prac   mer rider of a Beale Facile recalled
in a lette   *eshaker* magazine in 1956 that

as to st   s really beautiful for riding
without   asier than a modern bike. As
boys, we c   de down hills standing or
kneeling o   vithout hands.

The Otto Dic   vo wheels that were parallel
to one another   trangest of all the cycles
designed to redu   of sitting above a high
wheel. It was pate   b T. Otto between 1879 and
1881.

The saddle was ju above the centre of the axle between the two wheels. The pedalled cranks below were balanced against the saddle; they turned the wheels by means of pulleys and spring-loaded steel belts. Steering was done by slackening one of the belts so that one wheel went round faster than the other.

The B.S.A. Company made about a thousand dicycles and throughout the 1880s there were Ottoists, as they were called, riding them. Learning to keep one's balance, seemingly impossible, was said to be a matter of minutes, though steering downhill took longer to master. Ottoists claimed that they could put extra power into pedalling because their weight inevitably bore on the pedals, and that they progressed well against the wind because on meeting it they could get even more directly over the pedals.

But manufacturers could not seriously have hoped that any of these machines would attract the multitude of inveterate non-bicyclists. It was the safety bicycle of the late 1880s which did that—the safety with wheels of equal size and a chain to drive the back wheel.

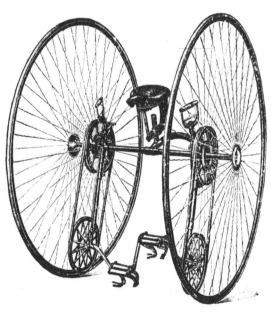

41   *Otto Dicycle, 1880*

Tricycles

On wood pavement, a well-made tricycle constitutes
one of the most agreeable, quickest and cheapest
means of transport it is possible to conceive.
Letter to *The Times*, 1882: subject, a
proposal to tax tricyclists.

The perils of the high-wheeler boosted sales of tricycles
—introduced commercially in the late 1870s. Tricycles,
as the advertisers were always pointing out, met the
requirements of elderly gentlemen, ladies and timid
persons. Their novelty gave them, too, a social cachet.
Sprigs of the aristocracy had no objection to riding
them. The Tricyclists' Association even sought special
privileges in the London parks on account of tricyclists
being better bred than bicyclists. In the early years
there was much scope for individuality in the choice
of machine: a summary of the many types to be had
appears later in this chapter.

Beside the high bicycle, the tricycle looked safe
indeed. Prospective riders saw that there was no need
to learn balancing and that they could remain mounted
even when the machine was stationary. One drawback
to the early tricycles, however, was that it was almost
impossible, in the event of a spill, for the rider to fall
clear of the enormous wheels. The files of newspapers
of the period are sprinkled with accounts of tricycling
accidents; in the year 1883 they appear to outnumber
the bicycling accidents. In July of that year *The Times*
thus reported the death, from falling off his tricycle, of a
young man aged 26, Walter Burrell, son of Sir Walter

42   *Tricycle carriage, 1881. 'A very suitable means of transport,' said* Cassell's Magazine, *'for those who are obliged to travel a great deal . . . light luggage such as most travellers require is supported behind.'*

Burrell of West Grinstead Park in Sussex:

> In returning from a cricket match on a tricycle close to the park, he was descending a hill when he endeavoured to reverse the action of his machine, and in so doing, it is believed, lost control over it and was precipitated from the tricycle upon his head, causing injuries from which he died after being conveyed to his father's house.[1]

At the date of this accident a favoured type of tricycle had driving wheels between forty and fifty inches high and a diminutive rear steering wheel which tended, perilously, to lose its bite on the road when going downhill. Sitting between those great wheels, the tricyclist rarely escaped a degree of injury from entanglement with the machine if he was overturned. Even on level ground, with no hill in sight, it was not difficult for a

[1] A stone cross by the roadside, inscribed 'Be ye therefore ready', marks to this day the site of the accident.

43　*Salvo Quad, 1880. Queen Victoria bought two.*

tricycle to tip over if it met a large stone. The fact that a tricycle makes three tracks to the bicycle's one is of only slight consequence on today's smooth roads: in the 1880s it meant two extra chances of encountering an awkward lump, rut or pothole.

In saying that Burrell endeavoured to reverse the action of his machine, *The Times*'s reporter meant that he was trying to back-pedal. Brakes, if fitted at all, were rudimentary and generally ignored in favour of backwards pressure on the fixed-wheel pedals. It could be an exacting procedure. To begin it when already going fast down a hill courted the unnerving mishap of losing one's pedals and the sudden feeling, as all revolved faster and faster, of being out of control. It was at such times, in the struggle to regain the pedals, that tricyclists became unseated, even when the way ahead was clear and the surface fairly smooth.

Richard Church once witnessed an accident to a

LIKE HIS CHEEK.

"'OLD YER 'OSS, SIR?"

woman tricyclist who lost her pedals and wrote of it in
Over the Bridge (Heinemann, 1955). He and his father and
brother were bicycling from London to a village in
Hampshire. Beyond Guildford, they had been followed
for some miles by a young stranger who seemed, rather
irritatingly, to be using them as pacemakers. They were
bent over their handlebars, at the bottom of a sharp
descent, when

> . . . suddenly we heard a cry of alarm. I raised my
> bemused head, and saw a stout woman on a tricycle,
> tearing down the hill with her feet off the pedals,
> which were flicking up and down, as it seemed, faster
> than the eye could follow. An instant later there was
> another cry from the stout woman, and a crash
> alongside us. The young man had pulled out, intend-
> ing at last to pass our slow cortège. But he chose the
> wrong moment, for the tricyclist went slap into him.
> Machines and bodies appeared immediately to
> multiply, and to be scattered all about us, amid a
> cloud of white dust, and groans and cries.

It turned out to be not too serious, the only physical
injury a grazed thumb for the young man. Mr. Church

45   *The Earl of Albemarle, president of the National Cyclists'*
Union, c. 1886

46   *Danger board, c. 1885*

senior lifted the woman up 'as though she were merely an inflated balloon', and helped her to the side of the road. He allowed her to relapse there into tears and hysteria, returning to her after he had bound the young man's thumb and reproved him for blindly turning out:

'Now, Ma'am!' he cried. 'Is nobody with you?'
She was still incoherent, but we could detect references to her poor husband, and demands for the police. . . . 'It's nobody's fault,' said Father, brushing away at her garments, and flicking her face and hands with her own handkerchief. 'You lost control. Should never do that, you know. Might have ruined your machine.'
   By this time the poor husband approached down the hill on a bicycle of rare vintage. . . .

Before improved brakes came in, it was not thought timid for bicyclists as well as tricyclists to dismount on coming to a downhill stretch of road. Largely through the efforts of Lord Albemarle, who became president of the National Cyclists' Union in 1883, danger boards were put up at the top of steep hills. They were solid plates of iron bearings the words *To Cyclists this Hill is Dangerous*. Within a year or two they were to be seen all over the country.

For the proficient and careful rider, a tour or journey by tricycle could be extraordinarily pleasant on the almost deserted roads of the late 19th century; those who enjoyed most this kind of travel took their time, and attended to the health and working of their tricycle with something of the care a wise man gave his horse.

The Rev. L. Meadows White, in an article called *Jottings by a Cyclist*, maintained that the tricycle, properly treated, was 'the safest high-speed vehicle on the road'. He saw no reason why there should be more accidents with the modern tricycle (he was writing in 1891) than with any other means of locomotion. But it was essential, he said, to know something of the centre of gravity and what was meant by stable and unstable equilibrium; and it was imperative that the machine should be kept in perfect order, all nuts and bolts being examined from time to time to see they were firm in their places.

In a manner reminiscent of George Borrow, the clergyman invited his readers to picture an ideal tricycling start from a nice inn. You awoke, he said, with a somewhat hazy idea of where you were, and as it dawned on you that you must be off in good time if you were to rest during the heat of the day, you sprang out of bed and looked out of the window.

Down below in the inn yard the ostler goes about his business, and the splashing of water and the sounds of horses' feet give signs of the returning life

of day. The sun shines down on the red-tiled roofs
of the little town in which you have put up. . . . The
air is filled with a soft haze, and overhead is a
cloudless sky.

Now come instructions bearing a marked resemblance
to the passage in Borrow's *Romany Rye* in which an old
ostler speaks of the manner in which 'a gentleman should
take care of his horse and self whilst engaged in a
journey on horseback':

Having dressed, you will at once pack your bag,
and make sure that everything is snug within, and
that nothing will rattle about on the journey. Just
inside the bag you will be careful to place a writing-
case, with postcards, the maps necessary for the
journey, perhaps a sketch-book, and certainly, either
there or in your pocket, the C.T.C. handbook. You
will then, bag in hand, make your way downstairs.
Having ordered breakfast, you will, to save time, go
into the yard and receive your machine from the
ostler. You next oil the bearings, clean off some of
the superfluous dust, spin the wheels, and see that
everything is in good running order; set the
cyclometer to zero, and lastly attach your bag to
the luggage-frame, and make all secure.
    Your machine is now ready, but your hands are
probably a sight to behold. You therefore indulge in
a wash, and by that time are informed that your
breakfast is prepared. You make a hearty meal, as
it is the first in the day; then after a few minutes
rest you mount your machine, and pass under the
archway into the street.

Meadows White's soothing prose switches to the use of
the first person plural, and in his company we find to
our delight that a freshening breeze is blowing in our
direction. We have therefore an easy day ahead of us,
and

for the first ten miles we speed along at a uniform
pace on a slightly undulating road. We are, we will
suppose, in one of the quiet rural districts of England

—perhaps on our way from London to the West. . . . There are no difficult hills, and the road is fairly smooth, and often shaded by trees. We have come ten or twelve miles since we started, and we expect to ride some twelve miles more before we reach our midday halting-place. There is plenty of time, and as it is hot we halt for a while . . . on a little bridge over a stream. Railways are miles away on either hand, and we are out of the track of ordinary travellers.

As lunch time approaches, we reach the brow of a hill and can see below us in the plain a small cathedral town. Before descending to it, down a moderate hill, Meadows White insists that we dust ourselves and check the brake to be sure of arriving in proper style. Then, with feet on the rests, we glide down the hill. 'This,' he observes, 'is a truly enjoyable way of entering a city.'

Tricycles had been the subject of isolated experiments since about 1845. The 'light' German Tricycle (1870) was simply a boneshaker with a pair of wheels running loose at the back instead of one. It was unsafe and 'only colourably a tricycle at all'—as people complained of a penny-farthing with two close-together back wheels when it won the Tricycle fifty-mile road race championship of 1880.

The Dublin Tricycle of 1876 was the first three-wheeler to be made commercially. It had a large rear driving wheel, thirty-eight inches high, and two small steering ones. The rear wheel was propelled by wooden treadles through a system of levers and rods attached to cranks. In the middle of the machine, well above the front wheels and mounted on coil springs, was a seat resembling a sketching stool.

The Dublin was followed in 1877 by James Starley's Coventry Lever tricycle. This also had a single large driving wheel and a treadle drive (which was later changed for a chain drive); but everything was differently arranged. The fifty-inch driving wheel was in the

47   *Tandem tricycles, c. 1885*

middle at the side; in front and behind it were two small steering wheels. These worked in unison. At first they were steered by a tiller and then later by a side handle operating a rack and pinion device. Riders derived a feeling of stability from the fact that a relatively large movement of the handle diverted the steering wheels only slightly. The seat was mounted on flat springs beside the driving wheel.

The number and variety of designs for tricycles appearing in the late 1870s demonstrated almost frenetic inventiveness. A number of basic problems had to be worked out. For example there was the disadvantage, with tricycles having two rear driving wheels, that when the machine was turned the outer wheel had a bigger curve to travel than the inner. In fact the latter ground to a halt during a sharp turn. The first solution was to arrange that one wheel only should be driven while the other ran loose on the axle.

Then came the important invention of the differential gear, a piece of mechanism which is employed today in every car and lorry in the world. It consists of a balance gear embodied in the axle and dividing the shaft into two parts. The effect is to allow one wheel to over-run the other on turning and yet to allow both wheels to take their equal share of·the driving power.

The story of how James Starley came to invent the differential axle is given as follows in Geoffrey Williamson's *Wheels Within Wheels—The Story of the Starleys of Coventry* (Bles, 1966). Starley had built a machine from two penny-farthing bicycles coupled together. There was a rod joining the two large front wheels and a brace of saddles fixed above it. The machine was called the Honeymoon Sociable.

One Saturday in 1878, according to an account by Starley's son William, Starley invited his son to join him on a demonstration run to Birmingham, a total distance of about 35 miles. After a short time, a time enlivened by some carriage horses they met getting into a panic, the machine showed a marked tendency to swerve, especially when going downhill. When they came to a rise known as Knightlow Hill they felt a temptation to dismount and push, but Starley refused to do this with jeering spectators lining the route and urged his son to pedal harder. William pedalled so vigorously that the extra impetus caused the machine to swerve into a ditch on Starley's side.

William's story has it that his father simply said: 'Find a dock leaf—my hands are stung all over'. A dock leaf was found and applied. Then Starley sat down by the roadside and rested his chin in both hands. He nodded vaguely when asked if he was all right. He was staring fixedly at the back wheels of the machine. Presently he took a scrap of paper from his pocket and drew a diagram: 'I've got it, Bill! What a dunderhead I've been not to see it before!'

He then explained to his son that of course the Honeymoon Wonder wouldn't work evenly except with two riders of equal strength. A man and his wife would just go round in circles. 'We've got to have an axle made in two pieces, with two bevel wheels in the middle. Then it wouldn't matter how hard we pedalled—the wheels would go round independently.' The pair then abandoned the trip to Birmingham and went back to Coventry. Starley kept his son up late sorting out gear wheels and other parts while he himself carved a wooden model of the new gearing arrangement he had invented. On the Monday, two days later, he caught the first train to London to see about taking out a patent.

The invention quickly led to the production by various firms of tricycles with two large parallel driving wheels. Some had the third wheel at the back and some at the front; in either case it was extremely small like the hind wheel of a high-wheeler bicycle. Some were propelled by levers with treadles attached and some by a heavy continuous chain and pedals.

Partly because rear-steerers did well on the racing paths, many of the early tricycles were of this type. They were found to go up hills and plough through rough ground more easily than machines with the tiny steering wheel in front. But the rear-steerers had certain insuperable disadvantages which made people frightened of them. Downhill—as shown already—the rear-steerer was most unreliable, since the rider's weight was taken off the steering wheel. Moreover, the latter could be lifted clean off the ground by an application of the brake (should there be a brake). On perfectly level ground the rider had to sit well back to get steady steering.

Starley himself had used his differential gear in the construction of a new tricycle which he called the Salvo Quad (1878). Its steering wheel, tiller operated, was in the front. For extra stability, there was a fourth small wheel in the rear (hence the 'quad'); but this was discarded on later models.

Two Salvo Quad tricycles were ordered by Queen Victoria on 18 June 1881, while she was staying at Osborne in the Isle of Wight. Her interest was aroused by seeing one during an afternoon drive, when she noticed that the flashing mass of spinning spokes, although operated by a girl, easily outpaced her carriage. The girl was in fact the daughter of Starley Brothers' Isle of Wight agent and was encouraged to ride the machine as much as possible as an advertisement. She could hardly have been more successful. Queen Victoria had her identity discovered and sent for her to give a demonstration of the tricycle in the grounds of Osborne House. The queen accompanied her order for two Salvo Quads with a command that the inventor should attend when delivery took place.

Starley duly made the journey from Coventry. In his book, *Wheels Within Wheels*, Mr. Williamson states that Starley afterwards wrote as follows to his wife:

One of Her Majesty's gentlemen was ready waiting for me and was very kind. He told me what to do and how to address the Queen. It seems funny but you must not say thank you to her. You have to say I am very honoured, Ma'am. He told me that as it was such a nice day Her Majesty would receive me in the lawn and when we got outside there she was sitting on a rug on a small garden chair by a round table that was covered with boxes, reading papers with someone who must have been her secretary I think. Two of her Indian servants were standing near-by and one of her ladies just behind her. I could see the tricycle under a tree and a lady and gentleman looking at it. My gentleman told me to wait a minute where I was and he went up to the Queen and bowed. She looked up and said something and he backed away a few paces and came to fetch me. He told me to stop when he did and to bow when he presented me which I did. She is a tiny little old lady but somehow you don't think of it when she is talking to you and her voice is deeper than you would expect. She said We are very interested in your tricycle Mr. Starley. The Prince Leopold thinks he may soon be able to ride one. You see His Royal Highness examining it now. And then he came over to stand by the Queen and she said to him, this is Mr. Starley who invented the tricycle and he was most pleasant and asked questions about my other inventions. Then the Queen said We believe you have sons working with you Mr. Starley and that is very nice for you. Good children are a great support in life. We hope Mrs. Starley enjoys good health. Then the lady-in-waiting handed her a little leather case and she held it out to me saying we wish you to have this memento of your visit to us.

I was quite overcome and bowed so low that I nearly toppled over as I said I am very honoured, Ma'am. Then the gentleman led me away and I was surprised and pleased when the Prince came along and asked me to explain the working of the tricycle to him. A servant was wheeling it behind. We found a nice level drive where I got on and was soon rolling along in fine style. He seemed very pleased with it and thanked me very kindly.

After that my gentleman took me to a small room where I was given some refreshments and told me that a carriage had been ordered to drive me back to Newport where I was staying. When I opened the case in the carriage there was a lovely silver watch with the Royal Arms engraved on the back. . . .[1]

One of the first results of this adventure was that the Salvo Quad became the Royal Salvo. There is no record of the Queen having mounted its high-perched saddle; certainly her purchase gave a great impetus to the tricycle industry. Within a few years tricycles had become fashionable in the highest places. Lord Albemarle, himself a tricyclist, wrote in 1886 for the Badminton Library's *Cycling* that there was not a crowned head in Europe who had not a stud of them—and plenty beyond Europe:

The Khedive of Egypt has several tricycles; one in particular, which I have had the honour of inspecting, is so covered with silver plating, that one can hardly see the black enamel it is supposed to

[1] Mr. Derek Roberts, editor of *The Boneshaker*, maintains that the letter was written later by a hand other than Starley's. However that may be, the letter has a ring of truth of its own.

adorn . . . some of the Indian princes possess vehicles which will hold their own, though after seeing the Khedivial state tricycle, I cannot affirm that they are pre-eminent. I have seen a picture in which the Maharajah of an Indian state, together with the British resident at his court and all the great officers of the durbah, are seated on tricycles at the gate of the palace, and gaze at the lens of the camera with the breathless attention usual on such occasions.

By the late 1880s there were so many different varieties of tricycle on the market that people found it hard to choose. The steering could be front, side or rear, indirect or direct. The drive, too, could be front, side or rear; and it could be ungeared or geared, single or double. There were several types of tricycle for two people—offering, in their day, as much pleasure as two-seater motorcars.

The first of the double tricycles had their saddles side by side and were appropriately called sociables. They were especially popular with couples for the ease with which they could talk together as they went along, and

49   *Thomas Humber and his partner T. H. Lambert, on a*
     Humber tandem tricycle, 1885

also for the amount of luggage that could be carried at
the back. The front wheel was the steerer, operated by
the rider on the offside only; there was a single chain
with balance gear (as invented by Starley); the pedals
on the inside, where the lady was expected to sit, had a
clutch action so that the feet could remain still while
going downhill.

Sociable tricycles were slow, however, and in the mid-
1880s were seriously rivalled by a tandem variety having
one saddle behind the other. The fastest of these tandems
was the Humber, illustrated here. In June 1885 two men
covered a mile on it in the brief time of two minutes
forty-seven seconds; they also did five miles in fourteen
minutes twenty-two seconds.

Riders of the Humber tandem sat on each side of the axle. The heaviest went at the back, since otherwise the machine was likely to tip forward; but as an extra precaution against this tendency, a tiny safety wheel was fitted to the front of the machine. The hind wheel did the steering and was controlled entirely by the rider at the back; its bite on the ground, it was said at the time, was 'rather more than just sufficient to enable the steersman to control the machine'.

Although tandem tricycles gave way in the late 1880s to the more efficient tandem bicycles, specimens of the former long continued to be seen on the roads—along with the high-wheelers of rural labourers and boys. George Bernard Shaw favoured a tandem tricycle. In 1899 a drawing was done of him riding it with his sister-in-law, Mrs. Cholmondley; he wore his knickerbockers and she the voluminous skirt of the time.[1]

The final form of the tricycle, a form which survives today, was a single-saddled machine with front direct steering and single rear-geared drive. An important example is the Humber-Cripper which appeared in 1884, getting its name from the fact that Robert Cripps was the first person to put it through its paces on a racing path.

The most convenient way of mounting was by stepping on the axle from behind; most models had some sort of guard for the purpose on the left-hand side of the axle. At first the bicycle-type steering was automatic in that a cam and spring brought the wheel back into the central position when the handle bars were released. But it was soon found that 'free-steering' was perfectly satisfactory.

Another change that soon set in was that the wheel base grew longer and the front wheel bigger; the rider was moved further forward and the larger-sized steering wheel took more part in carrying the load. The introduction of pneumatic tyres in 1888 enabled makers to lessen further the size of all wheels and to reduce the total weight.

[1] Maurice Collis, *Somerville and Ross*, (Faber and Faber, 1968).

50   *Carrier tricycle for newsvendors, 1885*

The use of the tricycle for carrying and distributing goods dates from 1884, when the *Evening Standard* took to having papers distributed by means of a Singer machine called the Carrier. Soon afterwards it was adopted by the Post Office—despite the postmaster general having stated in Parliament the previous year that tricycles were not adapted for parcel carrying. Post Office tricycles had a high, round-topped holder with separate compartments for heavy and light parcels.

The appearance of these official scarlet tricycles on the streets of London, alongside the heavily-laden newspaper tricycles, opened the eyes of businessmen. Lord Albemarle said that as a vehicle for business purposes

> the tricycle has even a larger future before it than the bicycle. It will carry a considerable quantity of luggage, and can be drawn up to the side of the street and left unprotected until the owner returns.

51 *Carrier tricycle for postmen, 1886*

The number of shopkeepers who employ the carrier tricycle for the purpose of distributing their parcels, or circulating daily supplies to their customers, is steadily increasing. . . .

By the early 1890s the Post Office was supplying its rural postmen with tricycles, the lever-steered kind with two enormous wheels in front and a small one at the back. As the load might equal the weight of the machine, it was often laborious work to get along the rutted roads of loose flints and other stones. Finally, around the turn of the century, the Post Office acquired safety bicycles (authorized to carry up to 56 lb.), but even so a round of, say, twenty-five miles was no sinecure. Pneumatic tyres were a mixed blessing to country postmen: the covers usually lasted about four months and in the meantime were subject to punctures that had to be mended in all weathers.

Tricycle cabs were a development much discussed in the late eighties. It was seriously predicted that London would shortly have a service of such cabs and that they would find their way through the traffic faster than any horse-drawn conveyance.

This issue was never tested. However, bath chairs with provision for pedalling at the back were manufactured by Starley and Sutton and sold in profitable numbers as Coventry Chairs. James Starley used one regularly himself when he became an invalid; his son drove. Coventry chairs became very popular in Harrogate. Lord Albemarle saw parties of three or four of these machines going along in company, the occupants talking together in comfort and the drivers encouraging each other up hills.

He met in a restaurant a woman who had just returned from an expedition in a Coventry Chair to Fountains Abbey, nine miles away. Asked whether the man had dismounted for the hills, she replied that she had not noticed.

The gradual decline of tricycling's popularity after 1895 was largely caused by the ease with which the new safety bicycles could be ridden. The elderly gentlemen and ladies no longer felt obliged to ride something with three wheels.

Safety bicycles

The safety bicycle—the familiar low machine with a chain drive to the back wheel—began to make a tentative showing on the roads in 1884. People said how ugly it was. At least six years were to pass before it seriously challenged the position of the slender high machine, which was firmly referred to as the Ordinary Bicycle.

Common objections to the early, solid-tyred safeties were that they vibrated more, that pedalling so near the ground allowed mud to splash over the feet and that the chain drive wasted power. Many predicted in 1886 that 'these geared-up safeties' would never entirely supersede the full-sized bicycle or the tricycle.

But no one denied their comparative safety. Even if the rider ran into a low wall it was unlikely that he would be tumbled forwards on his head. It was noticed, too, as models improved, that free steering (steering unaffected by the pressures of pedalling) was devoid of strain, and that the long wheelbase reduced the incidence of side slips and also allowed the carrying of more luggage—either at the back or over the front wheel. Safeties might not be as fast as high-wheelers on the racing path, but they were better at climbing hills and took the terror out of a fast downhill run.

The high-wheeler was still holding its own in 1890.

But the introduction of air-filled tyres, two years previously, was beginning to tip the scales in favour of the safety machine.

The first man to fit a bicycle with air tyres was John Boyd Dunlop, a Belfast veterinary surgeon. He began experimenting with tyres in 1888 when a doctor advised cycling for the health of his young son and remarked that the exercise would be more beneficial still if somehow ,the jarring could be reduced.

Dunlop first tried out a hosepipe filled with water, but results were unsatisfactory. Then he thought of air under pressure and proceeded to experiment with solid discs of wood. He nailed a pocket of linen round one of them and inserted a blown-up rubber tube. His idea at this stage was just to compare the bouncing and rolling properties of a wheel surrounded with a cushion of air with those of a wheel shod with the usual solid tyre. He found, of course, that the difference was as marked as the difference between a tennis and a cricket ball.

The next move was to fit more carefully-made tyres to a pair of tricycle wheels with wooden rims. Dunlop protected the canvas pocket containing the rubber tube with rubber strips on the running surface. A simple non-return valve was provided for inflation (but not deflation), and the complete tyre was stuck to the wheel with a rubber solution.

A secret trial at night by Dunlop's son was judged a success especially as to comfort, and Dunlop at once set about exploiting his tyre. Before long he fell in with a Dublin business man called Harvey du Cros and became a director of the Pneumatic Tyre Company which du Cros enthusiastically founded. The company took workrooms in Dublin.

The Irish-made pneumatic tyres of 1889 came in for plenty of criticism. With their bulging sides, they seemed deformities beside the slim solid tyres of the day; they punctured easily and were not detachable. They were also extremely expensive at £5 a pair.

J. K. Starley, nephew of James Starley, saw no future for them. The head of the Centaur Cycle Company observed that only theoretical advantages could be

52 *The Brighton coach, 1888*

adduced in their favour. *The Cyclist* opined that 'the new
tyre should last at least a season'.

When a pneumatic-tyre safety bicycle appeared on a
Belfast racing track, ridden by W. Hume, it was hailed
with derisive laughter. There was astonishment when it
outpaced all rivals. In September 1889 Arthur du Cros,
son of the chairman of the Pneumatic Tyre Company,
took the first pneumatic safety to London, proposing
to show off its performance in a race at the Oval for
which he had entered. But the organizers of the race had
decided, he learned on arrival, to ban all safety bicycles.
Du Cros's demonstration of the new tyre in London was
thus limited to his ride through the streets from Euston
Station to the Oval and back again. He recalls in *Wheels
of Fortune* (Chapman and Hall, 1938):

> Omnibus and hansom drivers, making the most of
> a heaven-sent opportunity, had the time of their
> lives; messenger boys guffawed at the sausage tyre,
> factory ladies squirmed with merriment, while even
> sober citizens were sadly moved to mirth at a
> comicality obviously designed solely to lighten the
> gloom of their daily routine.

53 *Safety bicyclist beats coach's time. London to Brighton and back, 1890. In Crawley*

Not until the spring of 1890 was the superior speed of the air tyre effectively demonstrated on English racing tracks (superior comfort was not in doubt). In September of that year they were strikingly advertised through their use by C. A. Smith in riding from London to Brighton and back in less than seven hours. He exactly followed the route of the Brighton coach and beat by nearly an hour the coach's best time of seven hours fifty minutes—achieved in 1888 with sixteen changes of horses. (It should be added that the coach record had also been beaten, less resoundingly, by a man on a safety with solid tyres.) At last the tide began to turn against high Ordinary bicycles. Attempts were made to stem it by fitting them, too, with pneumatic tyres, but to no purpose.

John Boyd Dunlop was not in fact the inventor of the air tyre, though at first he believed that he was and acquired a patent. An air tyre employing rubber and leather had been invented by Robert William Thomson,

54   *London to Brighton and back. On Clayton Hill*

a Scottish civil engineer, in 1845; it was several times tried out, with a degree of success, on the heavy horse-drawn vehicles for which, necessarily, it had been intended.

In the autumn of 1890 Dunlop was officially informed that his patent was invalid: all he had done was to apply the pneumatic principle, an existing invention, to cycles. Anyone was at liberty to make or deal in air tyres. Harvey du Cros, who had founded the tyre company on the strength of Dunlop's patent, was dumbfounded. Years later he said: 'The day of my meeting with the Thomson patent in the year 1890 was one of the most disagreeable of my existence'. However the worst did not happen, for shortly afterwards du Cros contrived to buy the important patent of Charles Welch for detachable tyres held on by wires: the Pneumatic Tyre Company prospered after all, and Dunlop, whose name is today a household word, made an adequate fortune.

The early years of the 1890s was a time of much time-wasting litigation over minor tyre patents, much of it barren. All that concerned the public, of course, was the fact that the pneumatic tyres in general gave their purchasers progressively less trouble. Whole new groups of people took to using the comfortable and convenient safety bicycle: those who had previously thought cycling beneath them, the old and the nervous, those who had believed their physique to be unsuitable. It was seen that unlike riding a high bicycle, length of leg was of no consequence on a chain-driven safety. Whether he was four foot in height or six, the rider could have a machine geared to suit him.

Safety bicycles fitted with the ever improving pneumatic tyres brought about a remarkable change in everyday life. By the middle of the 1890s it was obvious to all that a cycling boom was in progress. People of every social class wanted a bicycle, and existing factories found themselves unable to keep up with the demand. It was estimated in 1895 that the total number of cyclists of all kinds in the United Kingdom was one and a half million; the basis of the estimation was that only two and a half per cent joined the Cyclists' Touring Club.

As well as for the purposes of exercise and sport, for racing, touring and circulating in the parks, the bicycle had become an accepted conveyance for getting to social and business engagements. Dukes were as ready as artisans to get out their tool kits by the roadside and undertake the mending of a puncture.

Bicycles were being tended in the mid-nineties with the sort of care customarily devoted to horses. After a ride, every speck of dust or moisture was wiped from them; and at night they were brought inside the house for fear that night air might rust them. Sir George Darwin used to have the family bicycles slung up to the ceiling of the kitchen passage.

Mrs. William James reported in *The Book of Beauty* (c. 1895) that in fashionable circles the bicycle was so much an object to be cherished that no menial could be trusted even with the task of putting it into the guard's van when travelling. At home it would be kept, not in

Unwilling to give up horses altogether, Captain Pelham effected a compromise. His first appearance in the park created quite a sensation.

the stables or outbuildings, but in the hall. In the marble hall of Chelsea House, in Londonderry House, in Grosvenor House and in many other mansions the bicycle stand was now taken for granted.

It had become the exception, she went on, to see a bicycle with ordinary black or unembellished paint. Most men and many women had their machines painted in their own particular colours. Lady Huntingdon had hers done green with primrose lines; Miss Cornwallis West's colours were crimson and blue; Princess Henry of Plesse had a pretty white machine; no expense was spared in finishing General Stracey's bicycle painted in the red and blue of the Guards.

Meanwhile the high bicycle no longer seemed in the least 'Ordinary' and acquired the joke name of penny-farthing. To the infinite regret of the sporting public, the old favourite was well on its way to extinction—except among a few enthusiasts who made a cult of riding no other kind. One of the last high bicycles to be turned

56   *Lawson Bicyclette (a word later adopted by the French),*
      1879

out was the Rudge Ordinary of 1892 with a pneumatic
tyre on its fifty-six inch wheel.

Technical histories of the safety generally acknow-
ledge H. J. Lawson's Bicyclette of 1879 as the first design
for a bicycle with a chain drive to the back wheel. Its
front wheel is forty inches in diameter and the back
wheel twenty-four. The saddle is placed so far to the
rear, in the interests of safety, that the handlebar has
to operate indirectly through a link. Although the
Bicyclette is clearly descended from Macmillan's invention of 1839, there is also a likeness to the high-wheeler
in the size of the front wheel and in the frame consisting
of a single backbone. The Bicyclette was manufactured

57   B.S.A. Safety, constructed largely with tricycle parts,
     1884

in small numbers by Rudge, but proved a commercial
failure—it seems it was too much in advance of its time.

Several different safeties came on the market in 1884.
The B.S.A. machine and J. K. Starley's first Rover both
had indirect steering like the Bicyclette—even though
the larger wheel was behind and not in front. The Humber bicycle of 1884 sported a more advanced frame and
steering that was direct. But the front wheel was made
so small to reduce weight that handling was difficult on
rough ground.

The bicycle looked upon as the most interesting proto-
type of these years is the second of two Rover Safeties
designed by J. K. Starley in the year 1885. The great
majority of all bicycles made since then have been based
on it. In particular, it originated the strong compact
frame known as the diamond frame, which is still used.

As the illustration shows, the Rover has almost a

58 *J. K. Stanley's first Rover safety, 1884*

modern air, though of course the wheels are big by
present standards: the front wheel is thirty-two inches
in diameter and the back wheel thirty. A low total
weight of thirty-seven pounds (achieved, it is true, by
the absence of brakes or mudguards) is only seven
pounds more than the average weight of today's conventional roadster.

By 1886 several firms were producing bicycles based on
the Rover. Tests had shown that for the same expenditure of muscular energy, a person riding this type of
bicycle could cover about five times the distance that
could normally be covered on foot. Nevertheless, various
other designs were made up before the diamond-frame
arrangement became standard.

One of the most interesting of the intermediate types
was the Whippet spring-frame bicycle made by Lindley
and Briggs (1885). It was entirely practical. The chief

59   *Later versions of the Rover. Both 1885*

60   *Boy riding a Rover, 1885*

feature was that the relative positions of saddle, pedals
and handlebar did not alter: all three were built into a
rigid triangle isolated from the main frame by a strong
coil spring and a movable shackle in the steering mechanism. The Whippet sold well until the pneumatic tyre
proved a simpler and more efficient means of absorbing
road shocks than a spring frame.

A curiosity among safeties of this period was the
Geared Bantam. It was in fact a dwarf front-wheel-drive
machine with a geared up mechanism—and the last of
the front drivers except for children's bicycles.

The year 1890 saw the production of a diamond-framed
Humber bicycle barely distinguishable from bicycles
still running today. The Science Museum has a specimen
which successfully completed a journey of some 15,000
miles across Europe, Asia and America; the frame still
has the makeshift binding of telegraph wire with which

61   *Premier safety, 1885*

it did the last 1500 miles of the journey.

Bicycle expeditions of extreme length made the subjects of several books around the turn of the 19th century. Titles include *Over the Alps on a Bicycle, Across Siberia on a Bicycle* and *London to Pekin Awheel.* In the early years of the 20th century at least one school tried to brighten geography lessons with the aid of John Foster Fraser's *Round the World on a Wheel* (Methuen, 1899), an account of Fraser's bicycle ride of 19,237 miles across three continents.

The fact that bicycling was being taken up by the rich gave manufacturers a chance to experiment with very expensive bicycles that made use of new techniques now becoming available. The Dursley Pedersen, patented in 1893, was the first and most unorthodox of these superior models. M. Pedersen, who invented it, was a Danish engineer living in England; he invented,

62   *Whippet, 1885*

too, a folding bicycle for the Swedish Army.

The frame of his exceptionally light machine was completely triangulated, as the illustration shows, and consisted of light duplicated tubes. These gave the structure an increased torsional stiffness over the diamond frame of single tubes. The apices of the triangles were arranged to take the principal stresses; the saddle was slung between them like a hammock. The Dursley Pedersen was comfortable as well as light and went on being made till about 1914.

The first practical tandem bicycle appeared in 1886

63   *Raleigh safety, 1888*

and was the work of Dan Albone and A. J. Wilson. The frame was a single diagonal backbone which gave a low saddle at the back on which the lady was to sit. The first model—it was not made commercially—had coupled steering for both handlebars; but it was found that to share the steering was simply not possible, and one handlebar became a hand rest. As it was, there were often misunderstandings over the shared pedalling. Jerome K. Jerome writes in *Three Men on the Bummel* (Arrowsmith, 1900):

> It is the theory of the man in front that the man behind does nothing; it is equally the theory of the man behind that he alone is the motive power, the man in front merely doing the puffing. The mystery will never be solved. It is annoying when Prudence is whispering to you on the one side not to overdo

64   *Dursley Pedersen*

your strength and bring on heart disease; while
Justice into the other ear is remarking, 'Why should
you do it at all? This isn't a cab. He's not your
passenger,': to hear him grunt out: 'What's the
matter—lost your pedals?'

Tandems reached a satisfactory form in 1897 with the
introduction of a sturdy model by Raleigh.

Another type of bicycle for two people was the Sociable
bicycle, which had two saddles side by side and separate
pedalling gear. Balancing was something of a *tour de
force* and the vogue for this machine was brief. Some
believe it to have been the inspiration for *Daisy, Daisy,
give me your answer, do!* (1892), Harry Dacre's famous
song featuring 'a bicycle made for two', but it is much
more likely that Dacre had the ordinary tandem in
mind.

65 *Coasting on safeties, 1894*

The year 1896 was a phenomenal one for the cycle trade: agents hurried from factory to factory, cash in hand, pleased if they secured even a couple of machines out of the dozens they had on order. Gunsmiths and locksmiths deserted their trades for work in the booming cycle industry, which was backed by the investments of clergymen no less than financial adventurers. Then, the following year, a slump set in; and such was the degree of over-investment that the effects on many were disastrous.

The flow of orders for bicycles simply dwindled to a trickle, giving the impression that all who could buy a bicycle had already bought one and that those who had not done so aspired to one of the motor-cycles now being successfully produced. Although the reduced demand for bicycles continued, the machines made in the period 1900–1920 were gradually refined in matters of detail and in such ancillaries as the speed gear.

In fact certain bicycles of unsurpassed excellence were made in these years. The Golden Sunbeam by John Marston and Company had a reputation which has never been bettered. It was a machine with the standard diamond frame, but everything was of perfect quality; it had an oil-bath chain case and a two-speed epicyclic bracket-type gear. The model of 1902 remained practically unaltered for thirty-four years. No one could see how it might be improved.

There were, however, a few new ideas in this period. Some arose as a result of the use of bicycles on active service. A soldier-bicyclist in the Matabele campaign successfully transported over several miles four hundred rounds of ammunition weighing one and a quarter hundredweight while maintaining, for part of his journey, a running fight with natives. The B.S.A. Company made an ingenious folding bicycle for use in the South African War; and machines of similar design were produced in large numbers for the 1914–18 War.

An Army cyclist manual, in circulation at least until the start of that war, tells bicyclist battalions that when surprised by cavalry they should stand their machines upside down and spin the wheels to frighten the horses.

It would be interesting to know if there was ever a battle in which this was done.

Bicycles with shaft and bevel-gear were available between 1904 and the early 1920s; but they were never in great demand as they offered no material advantage over the cheaper and simpler kind driven by a chain. Indeed it can be said in general that such small developments as did occur in the first quarter of the 20th century did nothing to modify the standard form which the safety bicycle had reached by 1900.

Riding instructions

There is only one phrase to describe his [Mr.
Hoopdriver's] course at this stage, and that is—
voluptuous curves. He did not ride fast, he did not
ride straight, an exacting critic might say he did not
ride well—but he rode generously, opulently, using
the whole road and even nibbling at the footpath. The
excitement never flagged.
  H. G. Wells, *The Wheels of Chance*
  (Dent, 1896).

Mr. Hoopdriver was a draper's assistant and had with
difficulty taught himself to ride; he was just beginning
his first long journey. Learning to ride a bicycle was a
serious business in the 19th century; most of the learners
were adults with no previous experience of propelling
themselves on wheels. Just as today there are schools
of driving for motorists, so there used to be schools of
riding for bicyclists; and, according to a report of 1897,
such schools existed in most towns of any importance.
  It was not only the maturity of the learners that
brought about a demand for graduated half-hour lessons.
The bicycles in those days were more difficult to master.
The handlebar of the heavy, iron-tyred boneshaker had
to be braced against the side-to-side effect of pedalling
the front wheel; ill-judged step work on the high-wheeler
could lead to a foot getting amongst the spokes or a
grazed leg; to ride either of these machines—and the
early safety bicycles as well—called for a certain skill
in coming to terms with pedals which ceased to revolve
only when the machine was stationary. Even walking
his machine could bring the apprentice cyclist a bang
on the shin—until he had learned to keep clear of the
fixed pedal.

How to Ride a Velocipede or Boneshaker: 1869

The following instructions, the first of the kind to be
published, appeared in a booklet by Charles Spencer,
owner of the London gymnasium in which Rowley
Turner demonstrated a Michaux velocipede. He advises
learners who have no competent teacher at least to avail
themselves of a friendly arm:

First Lesson. Having become accustomed to the
motion of the machine [by wheeling it slowly about],
and well studied its mode of travelling, the next
thing is to get the assistant to hold it steady while
you get astride, and then let him wheel it slowly
along. Do not attempt at first to put your feet on
the treadles, but let them hang down. All you have
to do is to keep the front wheel straight with the
back wheel by means of the handles.

Second Lesson. Having pretty well mastered the
balancing and keeping the machine straight, you
may now take a further step, and venture to place
your feet on the treadles. You will find the novel
movement of the legs up and down liable to distract
your attention from the steering and balancing; but
after a few turns you will get familiarized with the
motion, and find this difficulty disappear; and it
will seem within the bounds of possibility that you
may some time or other begin to travel without
assistance.

Third Lesson. Now, having in the first lesson ridden
with the feet hanging down, and in the second with
them on the treadles, in the third lesson you should
be able to go along for a short distance, working the
treadles in the usual way. Of course for some time
it will be advisable for the assistant to walk by your
side, to catch you in case of falling. When you have
arrived at this stage, you only require practice.

To Get On and Off. The proper way is to vault on
and off, which is the easiest way of all, *when you
can do it*. At first, it may be from want of confidence

67 *Illustrations from the first manual for beginners*

how to commence practice

how to alight

how to rest

in yourself, you will jump *at* the machine, both you and it coming down.

Stand close to the machine, holding the handles firmly; then run a few steps with it to get a sufficient momentum, and then, leaning your body well over the handles, and throwing as much of your weight as you can upon them, with a slight jump throw your right leg over the saddle.

You must be very careful that while running by the side you keep the machine perfectly upright, particularly at the moment of jumping, or you may go right over it, and fall with it on top of you on the other side.

To get on with the help of the *treadle* is a very neat and useful method, but requires considerably more practice than vaulting. Stand with the left foot on the treadle, and taking a slight spring from the ground with the right foot, give the machine a good send forward and bring the right foot over the saddle. The secret of this movement is that you put as little weight as you can on the treadle, merely following the movement, which has a tendency to lift you. Keep the greater part of your weight on the *handles*.

Another way is by running by the side of the bicycle and watching the time when one of the treadles is at its lowest; then place your foot upon it, and as it comes up the momentum will be sufficient to lift you quite over into the saddle.

A capital way of alighting from the machine while in motion is to throw the right leg over the handle. You hold the left handle firmly, and raise your right leg over and into the centre of the handles. Then, lifting your left hand, you will be able to bring your leg over into a side-sitting posture and drop on to the ground with the same movement. This I consider one of the easiest methods of getting off. although it looks so difficult.

The illustration shows a very useful position when taking long journeys, as it rests the legs. Sometimes you do not require to work the treadle descending an incline. In this position the *break* is generally used; but, when putting it on, mind you do not turn the handles with both hands at once, but turn with first one and then with the other, otherwise when you let go to take fresh hold the handles will fly back to your great annoyance.

The most useful feat of all is to stop the bicycle and sit quite still upon it. Gradually slacken speed, and when coming to a standstill, turn the front wheel until it makes an angle of 45 deg. with the back wheel. Of course this is a question of balancing, and you will soon find the knack of it. When the machine inclines to the left, slightly press the left treadle, and if it evinces a tendency to lean to the right, press the right treadle until, sooner or later, you achieve a correct equilibrium, when you may take out your pocket-book and read or even write letters.

How to Ride a Penny-Farthing: 1877

Charles Spencer's instructions appeared in *The Modern Bicycle*, 1877. He considered that a rider 'of average height, say 5 feet 8 inches', should choose a machine with a wheel of 52 to 54 inches diameter.

The saddle being nearly as high as your shoulder, it is impossible to vault on; but a step is fitted on the backbone at a convenient height on the left. It is jagged to afford a firm grip for the toe. There are two ways of mounting. One is to start the machine and run by the left side, and put the toe upon the step while in motion, throwing the right leg over on to the seat; the other is to stand at the back of the machine with the left toe on the step and to hop with the right leg until you have gained a sufficient impetus to raise yourself on the step, and throw your right leg across the seat.

The first is the best plan. In many cases it is the only practicable way, as, for instance, for remounting on a slight ascent, where it would be most difficult to get up sufficient speed by the hopping plan. This,

AN AMBUSCADE.—Captain de Smythe insidiou-ly beguiles the fair Laura and her sister to a certain secluded spot where, as he happens to know, his hated rival, Mr. Tomkyns, is in the habit of secretly prac-tising on the bicycle.   He (Captain de S.) calculates that a mere glimpse of Mr. T., as he wobbles wildly by on that in trument, will be sufficient to dispel any illusions that the fair Laura may cherish in her bosom respecting that worthy man.

moreover, does not present a very graceful appearance.

Hold the handle with the left hand and place the other on the seat. Now take a few running steps, and when the right foot is on the ground give a hop with that foot, and at the same time place the left foot on the step, throwing your right leg over on to the seat. Nothing but a good running hop will give you time to adjust your toe on the step as it is moving. It requires, I need not say, a certain amount of strength and agility.

Having mounted the high machine, you will find that the reach of the leg, and the position altogether, is very different from the seat on the boneshaker; but when you get some command you will find the easy gliding motion much pleasanter, as well as much faster.

In alighting by the step all you have to do is to

reach back your left foot until you feel the step, and, resting upon the handles, raise yourself up and throw the right leg over the seat to the ground.

But I consider getting off by the treadle much the preferable way when you can manage it. First see that the left hand crank is at the bottom, then throw your right leg with a swing backwards and continue until you are off the seat and on the ground. As it is, of course, easier to get off the slower you are going, you must come almost to a standstill, just keeping way enough to prevent the machine falling over. If you attempt it when going at all quickly, you will have to run by its side after you are off, which is a difficult feat for any but a skilful rider.

The great advantage of getting off in this way is that you can choose your own time, which is very useful when an obstacle suddenly presents itself, as in turning a corner. In getting off the other way you are liable to lose time feeling for the step.

When you come to have any command over your machine, and have time to think about *style*, you cannot do better than take for your model John Keen, the champion, whose upright and graceful seat gives such an impression of quiet power.[1]

Ġ. Lacy Hillier, in *Cycling*, 1887, writes about precautions that can be taken against mishap.

A stout pair of gloves is a great protection to the hands in the case of a header, and when a cropper at high speed seems inevitable the rider should avoid as far as possible falling *against* banks or similar obstructions. A fair fall on the road, especially if the shoulder can be made to come first to the ground, generally results in a series of somersaults, which is nothing like so dangerous as a dead stop against a bank or wall.

It may seem absurd to offer hints how to fall, but it is quite an art of itself, for which many riders develop a peculiar talent. If the rider can by any little ingenuity twist or turn on to his back, the

[1] He rode twenty miles on a penny-farthing in an hour.

69 *Legs over handlebar for safe coasting on a high-wheeler*

resulting injuries will be very slight.

Down hill the safest position is without doubt that in which the legs are placed on the handle-bar, as not only will a sharp application of the brake bring the rider over the front wheel and on to his feet, but in cases of a bad fall the rider gets at once clear of his machine. All practical cyclists know that the most painful injuries are caused by the handle-bar striking the front of the legs.

Should a rider fall on the road, as soon as the first pain has gone off he should essay to move. If his machine is uninjured and the cause of the cropper— a stone for example—clearly apparent, he should get on at once and make for the nearest doctor. If, on the other hand, he suspects a broken spring or a damaged bearing he will do well to walk, but in any case he should move off at once ere his wounds get stiff. Careful bandaging and the application of vaseline on lint will enable him to get home, and warm water and a soft sponge should be courageously employed to extract the grit and dust from the wounded surfaces.

Lacy Hillier quotes a letter from G. B. Partridge on the subject of wounds received in bicycling:

> The best treatment undoubtedly is copious washing with warm water; it need not be desperately hot, and much of the foreign matter may thus be got rid of with the aid of a soft rag or sponge. Very often larger fragments more or less imbedded in the skin may be removed at the time with a needle point, and this will be a considerable gain as to speed of recovery. Large soft *linseed-meal* poultices will materially hasten the separation of particles too deeply imbedded for such mechanical treatment.

How to Ride a Safety Bicycle: 1897

A. C. Pemberton in *The Complete Cyclist* regretted that much nonsense had been talked by medical men about the 'constant mental strain of balance' to which a cyclist was subjected. However this might be for learners, for regular riders such a strain was non-existent. The wheels tended to keep themselves upright from centrifugal force.

What each learner must remember is simply to turn the handles in the direction in which he is falling. Having drummed this into his head, the rest is easy. He will soon discover that there is a happy medium and that the bars require only to be turned slightly, and instantly brought back to the straight as soon as the machine has resumed the perpendicular.

After a couple of lessons, say, of half an hour each, any average person should be able to ride for short distances. It is possible with a Safety to dispense with assistance, but not advisable. The process when no assistance is forthcoming is to obtain a low-built machine, and put down the saddle until the rider can easily reach the ground with both toes. He can then, on a gentle incline, allow the machine to progress of its own accord, helping it occasionally, à la hobby-horse, until he has mastered the difficulty of keeping it upright.

As soon as the rider can balance himself—or herself, as the case may be—frequent practice in mounting and dismounting must be indulged in until the feat can be easily accomplished under any circumstances.

The method of mounting for gentlemen, using one of the modern light bicycles made without a step, is to stride the machine with one foot on the ground, or, if it is too high for him, on a bank or curb, and to push off with this foot while with the other making a strong stroke with the pedal. Ladies having as a rule a shorter reach than men, it is requisite that the mount be made more from the pedal.The rider gets into position with one foot on the pedal, which should be placed at about one-third of its stroke on the downward grade. Then with a spring from the

70 *An adult's first lesson on a safety, 1894*

71 *Advertisement for an embrocation, 1890*

GREAT SELF-RESTRAINT.—*Lady in pony-cart (who has made several unsuccessful attempts to pass persevering beginner occupying the whole road).* " Unless you soon fall off, I'm afraid I shall miss my train ! "

other foot, aided by pressure applied to the descending pedal, she starts the machine.

Dismounting is easy. Men simply use the left pedal as a fulcrum, and, by swinging the right leg over the back wheel, step easily to the ground. Ladies dismount in a different manner. Owing to the open frame, it is possible to bring either foot over on the same side as the other. Remember to choose the time when the pedal is ascending; by placing their weight on it as they alight, they will check the remaining velocity of the machine, so that a dead stop is made.

To be a neat rider one of the first points to be considered is the acquisition of the art of riding straight without visible effort. Try and follow, if possible, any straight rut left by a cart in the road, and always endeavour to make as near a bee-line as possible. Riders who cannot keep straight do much harm to their machines, and often suffer from a plague of punctures. These are caused by the fact

73   *Advertisement of 1884*

that being always on the twist, they help any sharp substance to penetrate the tyre, in the same manner that a bradawl works in much easier when turned than when merely pushed.

Pemberton applauds the practice of certain continental cities of making learners pass an examination in proficiency.

It would be a good thing if the same regulations were in force in England. It would prevent many ambitious learners running into peril, and would quiet the tongues of many who talk loudly of the dangers of cycling.

How to Ride a Tricycle: 1883

The following hints appeared in *The Tricyclists' Indispensable Annual* for 1882 and for 1883. Most non-tricyclists, said the introductory paragraph, seemed to think there was nothing to learn about tricycling. Such, however, was not the case, for although a person could sit on a tricycle and propel it without falling off, it required some little skill to drive it through the streets and over the hills.

In steering do not give sudden and spasmodic twists to the steering handle, but turn it as gently, firmly and steadily as possible. When travelling fast be very careful to hold the steering handle firm, and to turn less sharply than on other occasions. Should a sudden turn be requisite by any unforeseen circumstance, take care to throw the body right over the inner wheel as you turn.

Take care to slacken speed considerably when desiring to turn sharply or to go round a corner. If this is not done a capsize is the sure result. Never attempt to turn sharply when going down hill. Take care and back pedal as well as use the brake until the bottom of the hill is fairly in view, and even then it is not well to take off the feet unless the machine is provided with one of the more powerful kinds of brake.

In ascending hills hold the handles firmly, get as
much purchase or pressure from the loins as you can.
You may vary this, and ease yourself by rising out
of the seat, steadying the body with your hands, and
standing upon the pedals, thus driving the weight
of the body. In doing this, allow the weight to be on
the ascending pedal, lifting the other leg so as to
keep the chain always in tension.

Don't sit on the machine like a log of wood, but
accustom yourself to accommodate yourself to its
sway in going over obstacles. A very deep gully or a
large stone is best taken by leaving the seat and
putting all the weight for the nonce on the handles
and pedals.

In encountering freshly laid stones, get off and
walk, as it saves the tyres, the weight of the rider
not being upon them. Always be courteous to way-
farers, both pedestrians and drivers of horses.

8

Women on wheels

Women joined in the hobby-horse craze and a few tried boneshakers. The high-wheeler was strictly for men. It was not only almost impossible to keep clear of spokes in the obligatory long clothes; the whole weight of late Victorian propriety set itself against the adoption by women of so masculine and revealing a posture.

Girls who contrived to get themselves astride a brother's bicycle felt they were doing wrong, or at least that they might be caught. However, a young lady who wrote to a magazine in 1885 about having used a bicycle (most likely, at that date, a high one) was rewarded with a measure of reassurance in the printed reply: 'The mere act of riding a bicycle is not in itself sinful, and if it is the only means of reaching the church on a Sunday, it may be excusable'.

James Starley, it is true, designed an ingenious ladies' version of his tall Ariel to be ridden in a side-saddle position, but it was so complicated, and hard to master, that few were actually sold. It had the handlebar lengthened on the side nearest the saddle and shortened on the other side. To counteract the bias of the rider's off-centre position the back wheel was mounted on an overhung axle.

The only form of cycling suitable for women, it was generally agreed, was tricycling. At first (in the early 1880s) they were constrained to do it in a most inefficient manner: the only ladies' tricycles were rear-steerers with a cushioned seat placed low down and at some distance from the pedals. The posture, intended to be decorous, was often in practice the reverse. Lacy Hillier, writing in 1886 of the first women tricyclists, had this to say:

> The dress was constantly riding up over the knees, each alternate stroke lifting it higher, and many attempts were made to design some method of keeping it in place. Some riders sewed a considerable weight of shot into the lower edge, whilst others fastened the front of the skirt to their boots or shoes, with the very obvious result that the skirt dragged over the knees and rapidly tired the rider.

Men as well as women experimented with ways of overcoming the difficulty and a remedy was found: the dress was left alone, it was the position of the rider which changed. Instead of having her seated low down, she was given an upright position over the pedals of a front-steering machine. A saddle was offered. At first the ladies refused to use this and insisted on a seat as before; but in due course discomfort won them round.

Instead of awkwardly rising and falling in front of the body, the ladies' knees now moved as though in the action of walking. As Lacy Hillier put it, 'The skirt was simply thrown out by either knee alternately, and still hung gracefully and comfortably in front'.

The Cyclists' Touring Club, formed 1883, discussed very seriously the dress that should be adopted by lady tricyclists and, following a meeting in February 1884, published recommendations in its official gazette. Among them was a woollen garment for next to the skin; a pair of dark grey woollen stockings; a pair of loose knickerbockers fastened with elastic (or by a cloth strap or buckle) under the knee or, as an alternative, a pair of trousers cut loose to just below the knee and thence tighter down to the foot; a plain skirt, with-

Shawswater

MAKE SMART *Dress Fabrics*

Cycling, Golfing, Fishing, Shooting, and "Every-Day" Costumes.

THE DRESS GOODS·FOR THE SEASON.

These high-class fabrics neither cockle nor shrink. They are unaffected by weather or climatic influences of any kind, and their colours are guaranteed fast dyed. While always retaining a most stylish appearance, they will stand any amount of wear and tear and, in choiceness of design, are absolutely unrivalled. LADIES should send to us for Patterns, which are sent on approval Post Free to any address. We have an immense variety in the newest styles, and cut pieces to any length required. The Shawswater Dress Fabrics are also most suitable for Gentlemen and Children's wear.

FLEMING, REID & CO., SPINNERS & MANUFACTURERS. ⟩ THE WORSTED MILLS, Greenock, N.B.

74   *Advertisement of 1895. See on p. 141 how a woman could be deformed by fashion*

out pleats, of sufficient fullness to allow absolute freedom of movement; a bodice or jacket cut either to fit the figure or of Norfolk shape, lined throughout, including sleeves, with flannel. A smallish hat was considered advisable—with some provision for the protection of the neck and eyes: large hats caught the wind. Propriety was assured with knickerbockers or trousers (themselves outer garments) beneath a full-length skirt.

All lady tricyclists were advised at this date to choose a grey material. One reason, said Lacy Hillier, for

> the protection which ladies undoubtedly find in the C.T.C. uniform lies in the fact that it is so little remarkable, and so closely resembles that ordinarily worn by the wife of the parson or doctor.

The tricycle remained the only machine for a respectable woman till about 1890. Women with an urge to learn the art of balancing on two wheels practised in secluded gardens, or early in the morning when no potential spectators were about.

The first hint of revolution on the way showed itself in the popularity of tandem tricycles on which women took the front seat and were under masculine convoy and protection. Gradually a few two-wheelers with dropped frames appeared on the market, but even these safety bicycles were thought too improper and dangerous for ladies to ride. They were expected to stick to their tricycles. Gwen Raverat, writing of this time in *Period Piece* (Faber and Faber, 1952) says that her mother had a lady's tricycle when they lived in Cambridge and she herself a child's model:

> we used to go out for family rides, all together; my father in front on a bicycle, and poor Charles standing miserably on the bar behind my mother, holding on for all he was worth. I found it very hard work, pounding away on my hard tyres; a glorious, but not a pleasurable pastime.
>
> Then, one day at lunch, my father said he had just seen a new kind of tyre, filled up with air, and he thought it might be a success. And soon after that everyone had bicycles, ladies and all. . . .

Between 1894 and 1895 the situation changed overnight, as it were. *Punch*, underlining the obvious in the homely way it used to have, printed these verses called *The Biker Biked:*

Henpeck'd he was. He learned to bike.
'Now I can go just where I like',
He chuckled to himself. But she
Had learnt to bike as well as he,
And, what was more, had bought a new
Machine to sweetly carry two.
Ever together now they go,
He sighing, 'This is *wheel* and woe'.

In the 1895 edition of the Badminton Library's *Cycling*, ladies were actually urged to give up tricycling. The lady's rear-driven safety, said Miss L. C. Davidson, in a chapter called *Cycling for Ladies*, was much lighter and more easily pedalled than any tricycle; mounting was simpler and more graceful; dismounting was easy even when the machine was in motion; only one track was made, allowing the rider to pick her way along bad roads where a tricyclist would be forced to dismount; there were no lateral jars or twists, since obstructions were encountered in the central line of the machine; adequate braking power was available. Moreover, said Miss Davidson, the safety bicycle tended to be more free from danger.

If a lady is thrown from a tricycle, it is almost impossible for her to fall upon her feet, as the driving wheels are in the way, and a free escape would be impossible. On the other hand, in the case of a side slip, or any similar accident, on a Safety, the chances are very much in favour of the rider alighting on her feet.

But all too often lady bicyclists, hampered by their voluminous clothes, did not land on their feet. Gwen Raverat writes in *Period Piece:*

My mother must have fallen off her bicycle pretty often, for I remember seeing, several times, the most appalling cuts and bruises on her legs. But she never

DIVISION OF LABOUR.—It is not the business of ducal footmen to clean the family bicycles. The ladies Ermyntrude and Adelgitha have to do it themselves.

complained, and always kept these mishaps to herself. However, the great Mrs. Phillips, our cook, always knew about them. . . . She used to draw us into the servants' hall to tell us privately: 'Her Ladyship had a nasty fall yesterday; she cut both her knees and sprained her wrist, and the front wheel of her bicycle is bent all crooked. But don't let her know I told you.' So we never dared say anything, even if we saw her Ladyship limping.

Bicycling had become smart; lords and ladies had their pictures in the papers, riding along in the park in straw boater hats. But the problem of dress remained for a long time yet. At first girls had to wear baggy knickerbockers under their frocks—a costume which Mrs. Raverat and her friends thought 'horridly improper'. Apparently it felt less improper when at length the leg-concealing knickerbockers could be put aside.

Fashion writers were able to gloss over the obvious disadvantage of bicycling in a long skirt, because the improved safety bicycle had a guard over the chain and another over the spokes of the back wheel. In fact it was possible with care to ride decorously to a garden party in dress suitable for the occasion.

'The whole secret of a woman looking well on her bicycle', writes Mrs. Harcourt Williamson in *The Complete Cyclist* (1897), 'lies in the cut and hang of her skirt.' The best skirt of all, in her opinion, was made on the same lines as a habit, fitting the figure perfectly and cunningly stretched and shrunk. Once the skirt was successfully negotiated, the rest of the attire was simple. She goes on:

> Few women ride more gracefully than Mrs. W. H. Grenfell. I have seen her dressed all in soft green, a tweed skirt and velvet blouse, with gold belt and velvet Tam-o'-Shanter, looking more distinguished than anybody else as she passed through the throng in Hyde Park. At Battersea, which was always the most fashionable venue, Lady William, always neat and well-dressed, looked her very best in navy blue, with a white sailor collar and cloth toque. . . . I have seen black look very well on a bicycle. Mrs. Arthur Paget has a wonderful skirt—made in America, I think—which makes her look even slimmer than she is; and many women look their best in white—for instance, Lady Warwick, who wears an all-white costume, with white hat and gloves and shoes to match her white machine. Lady Archibald Campbell is generally dressed in drab, and her smart machine is painted to match. After all, however, the skirt is the thing, and once having this perfect, there is no reason why one should not wear an elaborate blouse and really smart hat on a fine day.

As well as paying attention to the appearance of their dress—and their bicycles—society ladies often prided themselves on their riding skills. Mrs. Harcourt Williamson wrote that Lady Cairns was a very plucky rider:

> One hears of her in the neighbourhood of Windsor flying down-hill with two or three companions as daring as herself, all hand-in-hand, and not one of

Winny (one mile an hour) to Annie (two miles an hour).
"Scorcher!"

77 *Skirt caught in mechanism, c. 1890*

them even attempting to guide their machines, but
trusting entirely to balance. The very good riders
all pride themselves upon being able to ride without
touching their handles; and Miss Muriel Wilson,
another smart cyclist, has been seen again and
again in Hull with one hand thrust into her coat
pocket and the other engaged in holding up her
parasol.

One wonders how such feats could be achieved in long
skirts; but on these convention insisted, despite the fact
that in almost every accident to women cyclists the
cause was entanglement of flying draperies in the
mechanism. It is hard today to imagine the fatigue of

78 *Rational dress on a tandem bicycle, 1894*

riding a fair distance in a wind-catching dress whose weight and friction were felt with every turn of the pedal.

But even in the early nineties a few lady bicyclists were defying convention; they took the bold step of abandoning skirts altogether. Some of them, in the teeth of ridicule and worse, adopted bloomers—that is, baggy pantaloons worn with a knee-length skirt. Bloomers were an American invention of the 1850s and so named after Amelia Bloomer who praised their usefulness in a magazine she edited called *Lily*. A practical outfit for women known as Rational Dress was the only one to meet with a measure of favour in England. It originated on the Continent in 1893 and consisted of

Vicar's Daughter: " Oh, Withers, your mistress tells me you are saving up to take a little shop and look after your mother: I think it is such a sweet idea! "

Withers: " Well, yes, miss, I did think of it; but now I've got the money I've changed my mind, and I'm going to buy myself one of these 'ere bicycles instead ! "

knickerbockers, long leggings and a coat long enough
to look feminine but not long enough to interfere with
movement.

The Lady Cyclists' Association, formed in 1892,
strongly defended rational dress; and in a surprisingly
short time it became acceptable for women engaged in
serious touring. Miss Davidson reported in 1895:

> In even the most remote parts of the kingdom, the
> sight of a woman on a bicycle has ceased to attract
> attention. Wearers of Rational Dress have made
> tours throughout the country, entirely unattended,
> and have received neither uncourteous notice nor
> annoyance.

All the same, the landlady of an Ockham (Surrey) hotel
was taken to court a year or two later—at the instigation
of the C.T.C.—for refusing to serve lunch to a woman
bicyclist, one Lady Harberton, because she was wearing
knickerbockers. The landlady was acquitted; but the
case was later celebrated as an important milestone on
women's road to emancipation.

Where, it might be asked, did the ladies of the nineties
go to on their bicycles, or tricycles, the ones who were
not undertaking long tours, circulating socially in one
of the parks or travelling to garden parties—or, with
male escort, to a new kind of cycling entertainment
called the illuminated musical ride? Large numbers
were already using bicycles to get to work, women office
workers and shop assistants wending their way each
weekday morning from the suburbs to the town. They
found the bicycle a convenient form of transport for
distances up to, say, ten miles. It was faster than the
horse bus, just as today it is often faster than the
continually-stopping motor bus. It also offered agreeable
feelings of independence.

For the army of women, unmarried as well as married,
who had no paid work to do and, at the least, one servant
to cook and do housework, a usual object for a bicycle
run was a local lending library or a shop that sold ribbon
or postcards. Respectability was demonstrated by the

custom of clergymen's wives and daughters bicycling
on their rounds.

Bicycles, writes Mrs. Raverat, recalling life in the late
1890s,

> gradually became the chief vehicles for ladies paying
> calls. They would even tuck up their trains and ride
> out to dinner on them. One summer evening my
> parents rode ten miles to dine at Six Mile Bottom;
> their evening clothes were carried in cases on the
> handlebars; for of course you couldn't possibly dine
> without dressing. . . . But when my mother came to
> dress that evening she found that, though the bodice
> and train were there, the skirt had been left behind.

But many women used their bicycles not so much to
get anywhere as to get away. The sensation of speed was
delightful and the unaccustomed exercise it entailed
seemed to do them good. Like going out on horseback,
just pedalling about made an event in the day; and like
the car that was soon to come, the bicycle offered a
soothing diversion, an escape into calmness from what-
ever might be going on at home.

It certainly hastened big changes in manners. The
beginning of bicycling was the beginning of the end of
the chaperone; and here and there a young girl found it
possible to act as suggested in some anonymous verses
after Marlowe, *The Passionate Cyclist and His Love:*

> Come ride with me and be my love,
> And I will all the pleasures prove
> Of sauntering in the shady lanes . . .

Mrs. Harcourt Williamson was alarmed about the way
girls would bicycle by themselves along miles of
deserted country roads:

> . . . parents and guardians will probably only become
> wise after the event. Given a lonely road, and a
> tramp desperate with hunger or naturally vicious,
> and it stands to reason that a girl, or indeed any
> woman, riding alone must be in some considerable
> peril.

9

Sensible precautions

It was largely because the early riders on their tall machines felt self-conscious that they paid what now seems an excessive amount of attention to their dress. The Cyclists' Touring Club issued many and earnest recommendations which in due course affected the cycling clothes of members and non-members alike.

By 1887 Lacy Hillier was able to write that the correctly dressed cyclist, especially if he adopted the neat C.T.C. uniform, was so common an object that he passed without special notice. Every day, he said, the public became more and more used to the sight: 'The familiar grey dress of the lady rider [on a tricycle], and the knee breeches, stockings, and short jackets of the sterner sex, occasion no remark'.

For the outer garments of the correctly dressed man, the Cyclists' Touring Club, assisted by 'a jury of experts', recommended—and sold—a West of England tweed with a small check pattern in grey. It did not show the dust, they said, and would stand any amount of knocking about: it would also wash, an important point as the bicyclist was apt to come in contact with oily parts of his machine. Those who wanted to get the greatest possible amount of wear from a uniform would do well

80 *Humber Cripper ridden by George Lacy Hillier,
wearing C.T.C. uniform*

81 *Correctly dressed late-Victorian bicyclists appropriately dismount. But note how they take up the whole road*

to have it braided, but instead of braiding it on the outside, which looked conspicuous, it should be braided inside, down the seams and across the breast to the buttonholes.

The jacket for bicycling should just reach below the saddle; for elderly tricyclists it could be cut a little longer. It should be single breasted and cut high up round the throat. The bottom of the front of the jacket should be cut away in two curves to stop it rubbing against the steering head and getting oily.

The question of knee-breeches or knickerbockers was a vexed one. However, riders with over-developed calves were advised to tone them down with wide baggy knickerbockers, and those with attenuated limbs to encase them in closely fitting knee-breeches. In all cases the nether garments, as they used to be called, should be worn well braced up, for a fold of cloth was likely otherwise to catch on the back of the saddle and cause a fall while the rider was trying to mount. Over-tight bracing, on the other hand, would cause endless discomfort and induce the rider to take up a stooped position.

THE LINE OF BEAUTY.

Athletic. "Don't you Bicycle?"

Æsthetic. "Er—no. It developes the Calves of the Legs so! Makes 'em stick out, you know! So coarse! Positive deformity!!"

The experts warned beginners of the danger of carrying certain objects in jacket pockets. Keeping a spanner in an inside pocket was particularly unwise, since in the event of a fall on the chest the spanner might cause a broken rib.

For headgear, the deer-stalker type of hat was considered the most generally serviceable. A good wide brim was an essential in a cycling hat, and it should be light, well ventilated and durable. If a felt hat was chosen, it should be a soft one and either the same colour as the coat or quite distinct from it. A light grey or brown was thought suitable for summer wear. In practice, however, most men wore light cricket or golf caps.

Boots versus shoes was a subject of long debate. In the end the shoes won. The advocates of boots were persuaded that since the weight of the body was carried by the saddle, there was no need for the ankles to be supported, and that the foot was best left entirely free to carry out the ankle actions involved in pedalling.

The idea of bicycling, like that of hunting, became so acceptable in the late 1890s that the appropriate male uniform was admired for its associations. *Punch*, in about 1895, published a 'dialogue between two young gentlemen', drawn into conversation through noticing that each was dressed in 'knickerbocker suits, gaiters and golf caps'. One remarks: 'They say in Paris that no one should become an habitual cyclist without medical authorisation'. A shortened version of the ensuing dialogue runs like this:

Yes. Quite right. Then when you are permitted, you ought to travel at a moderate pace. About five miles an hour is quite enough for a beginner.

Enough! Why, too much! You should 'gradually acquire speed'; not rush at it.

I read in the *Lancet* only the other day that merely increasing the pace of a bike a couple of miles an hour was sufficient to send up the normal pulse rate to a hundred and fifty!

Most alarming! And yet I can see from your costume that you are a cyclist.

Not at all. I am pleased with the costume, and, like yourself, have adopted it. I have never been on a bicycle in my life.

No more have I.

The young men need not have been hypochondriacs, for there was nothing unusual in being familiar with the medical jargon. Millions of words were written in the 19th century—and not only in the *Lancet*—on the effect of cycling on health. Moderate use of high-wheelers and safeties, unlike that of boneshakers, was not generally held up as injurious to the health. Discussion revolved, and not without justification, round the effects of immoderate use: men of all ages tended to use their bicycles and tricycles in a spirit of competition, and proudly made notes of their mileage. They used them as later on cars were used, for visiting friends two counties away, for boasting of having done eighty miles in a single run, or kept up sixty miles every day for a week. It was not unusual for imprudent riders to become ill through over-exertion. Some had a weakness to start with, of heart or lung perhaps, and became worse.

Not always, however. In 1883 *The Times* published a letter from a man who stated that although he had suffered for twenty-five years from a spinal infection which made it impossible for him to undergo a journey by train or coach, he had just completed a tricycle tour through Sussex of a hundred and fifteen miles. Throughout the trip he had not only been better in health, but had felt fewer pains than at any other period during the previous quarter of a century. The Badminton Library's *Cycling* reported the case of a man of 83, crippled with rheumatism, who decided to try the exercise of tricycling. During a period of several weeks at Hitchin he enjoyed daily rides, some of great length, and at the end of the time it was found that 'he had actually developed fresh muscle, a thing almost unheard of in one of his years, while his general condition could only be described as perfect.'

The two-volume *Household Physician* of c. 1890 rightly urged caution on the public. Although a healthy man could do sixty miles a day on a high-wheeler, or forty on

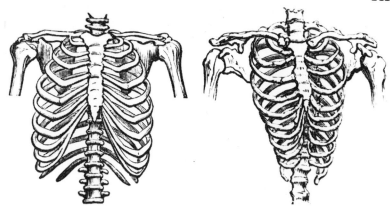

83 *Cautionary drawings published c. 1895. Above: how years of tight lacing altered a woman's skeleton. Right: a warning to the bicyclist*

RESTORATION of BRITISH CYCLIST.
20ᵗʰ CENTURY.   BRITISH MUSEUM.

A WARNING TO ENTHUSIASTS.

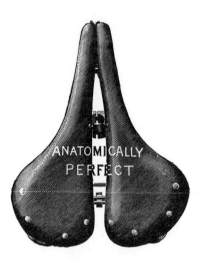

84   *Hygienic saddle, c. 1895*

a tricycle, the exertion of greatly exceeding these distances and keeping them up day after day, could not but be injurious to the health. Cycling, it said, had much value as a means of healthy exercise, but there was a great temptation to put on speed and to cover startling distances in the minimum of time. 'Anyone who has seen a young man dismount from his bicycle with every vein of his face and head standing out, and with his face turgid with exertion, and purple from deficient respiration, does not need to be told that in this exercise, as in others, the pace may kill.'

The vibrations of bicycling, it went on, by stimulating

THE BICYCLE FOR 1880.

THE ACME BICYCLE COMPANY'S
NEW AND SPECIAL LIST FOR 1880
NOW READY.

The A B C Bearings for 1880.

These Bearings are not only for 1880, but for all time.
For the first time a Bearing is perfected, which has a simultaneous adjustment on all
the bearing points, and this without the removal or addition of a single part.

The A B C Bearings for 1880
are applied to the back wheels of Bicycles, and to the hubs of Tricycles.

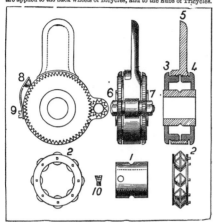

The A B C Bearings for 1880
Are applied to the pedals in a new and original manner. They have no projections, and
are always in the right position for mounting. These new Pedals can be supplied
separately for any Bicycle.

The A B C Bearings for 1880
Are supplied to the Trade, and all of them may be applied to any style of Bicycle.
They are all absolutely Dust-proof.

CHIEF DEPÔTS :

144, HIGH HOLBORN, and 144, CHEAPSIDE, LONDON.

Price Lists of new Bicycles, with all the newly-Patented Improvements,
Post Free on application.

---

the abdominal organs, were useful in certain sluggish
states of the bowels; but the bicycle should not be
mounted by anyone with heart or lung affections or with
a tendency to hernia.

Other authorities attributed numerous ills—a bad
liver was one—to the vibrations experienced in cycling
over rough surfaces. As a result several ingenious
saddles were tried out with a view to lessening the
shocks. The Hygienic Saddle was well spoken of: its
front part was divided and the division carried right
forward to the end of the peak so that the rider's weight
rested on his ischial tuberosities alone. Another kind of

saddle, the Anatomical, was shaped to the form and had no peak at all. The first of the form-fitting saddles is believed to have been devised by Starley. He sat on a heap of wet sand, pointed at the imprint left by his buttocks and said to the workmen: 'There, that's the shape a saddle should be.'

Continued talk of the dangers of vibration stimulated E. B. Turner, an experienced athlete and cycling enthusiast, to carry out in person a series of experiments. The results were published in *The Cycle* and showed, it was put forward, that nearly all the discomforts that arose after hard riding on bumpy roads were 'caused by over-exertion and were mainly local'. The so-called symptoms of vibration were simply those of fatigue-fever caused by the intoxication of the system by the product of its own waste. The provisions of nature for protecting the central nervous organs were too complete and well designed to be thrown out of gear by the puny shaking of a modern velocipede. 'Let no man be deterred from conquering the bicycle,' said the article, 'by dread of the slight vibration he must experience in riding it'.

It was the tricyclists, the more staid riders, who tended to worry about such matters and follow the health hints in the Press about the effects of pedalling. The riders of the high-wheel bicycles had simply gone ahead; few suffered in any way, except from falls, for the reason that to ride these tall, unstable machines at all it was necessary to be either young or agile and healthy. To these the stream of admonitions came to centre round the dangers of getting chilled. To publish advice on avoiding chills, a late Victorian did not need to be connected in any way with the medical profession. The Rev. G. Herbert, contributing to *Outdoor Games* (The Religious Tract Society, 1892) explained that bicycling brought every part of the body into play, causing a rider to perspire freely. It was therefore necessary, he said, that the *whole* of the garments worn should be made of wool—just as necessary as in football or rowing.

The undergarments should fit close to the body, he went on. With outer garments, designed of course to be inconspicuous, unlike cricketing and boating costumes, great care had to be taken to see that the linings and so on were all made of woollen materials; for tailors had a way, even when special orders had been given to the contrary, of putting canvas stiffeners in the bands of the trousers and other places. All these were liable to cause a chill. He himself was extremely particular:

> I make a rule now of opening the linings of my cycling clothes when they come from the tailors with my penknife, and examining the material placed out of sight. Too much care cannot be taken in this respect. Old and experienced cyclists go so far as to wear only those braces that are made of a woollen material.

Lacy Hillier was equally emphatic about the need for wool, without the least admixture of cotton or linen. As well as severe colds, he said, some bad cases of inflammation of the kidneys had been traced directly to the wearing of a linen waistband in the knickerbockers. Such ailments often attacked elderly tricyclists who insisted on riding in 'an old pair of ordinary nether garments':

> Sore throat is often to be traced to the linen band which so many tailors and shirtmakers will fit round the neck of a flannel shirt, whilst there is often in addition a little square of linen marked with the maker's name and address, which, when it is damp, can be readily felt, especially if the wind blows up coldly after a long run as evening falls.

When clothed from head to foot in pure woollen garments, said Lacy Hillier, the rider might get wet through half a dozen times and yet be safe from the worst results that could follow from cycling. Young riders might scoff, but experienced ones would simply advise them to wait until two or three weeks on a sick bed should have convinced them of the folly of casting aside as useless the experiences of their predecessors.

The bicycling mania that set in after 1895 gave genuine cause for anxiety: the new safety machine with its air-

L

filled tyres was so much easier to ride that all sorts of people took to bicycling who had previously thought it beyond them. Some were quite old and some far from physically fit. But troubles arose not so much because of their age or condition as because nearly everyone bicycled too long and too strenuously, racing against themselves if not others, clocking up on each run a prearranged number of miles. There was nothing hysterical in the publication in 1896 of Dr. George Herschell's book *Cycling as a Cause of Heart Disease*. This is how he saw the situation:

> To the artificial life that we lead in our big cities . . .
> we can trace the beginnings of many affections.
> Insufficient exercise apparently being in most cases
> a principal factor, we rush to the cycle as an easy
> and convenient method of undoing or preventing
> such mischief. What is the consequence? We fall in
> love with the machine, with its easy and agreeable
> motion: we give as much of our time to it as we can
> afford: we get rid of our dyspepsia, and in its place
> produce chronic degenerative changes in our heart
> and arteries. Indigestion, gout and neurasthenia
> diminish, only to be replaced by more serious ills.

He gives numerous examples of abuse of the bicycle which forced riders to abandon the exercise entirely. At the same time he emphasizes that 'cycling in moderation for moderate distances cannot be anything but beneficial for young and healthy adults'.

A man of 64, he writes, took up tricycling (the year was 1884) and after about three weeks' experience undertook to ride from Brighton, where he lived, to London. He managed to accomplish the task, but shortly afterwards became unconscious and died the next morning. Another, aged 41, who had been going for long, after-work, evening rides for ten years, always pedalling along as fast as he could, found one day that he could go only a little way before getting out of breath. A man of 31, complaining of severe palpitations, said he had been riding his bicycle constantly for several months, covering on average sixty miles a day for three days a week.

A well-built but pale and anxious-looking man of 41, complaining of pain across the chest while bicycling, had ridden almost every day for the previous five years; his favourite run was from London to Ditton and back.

Headache, vertigo and faintness, said Dr. Herschell, were commonly the first things which drew the attention of the cyclist to all not being right with him. . . . But enough has already been made of Dr. Herschell's observations to illustrate the way some doctors regarded the problems arising from the great cycling craze. At least the coming of the motor car offered a mode of travel more suitable for those who were neither young nor entirely healthy.

10

The foot-rest era

The parts of a cycle which riders had always to remember were the bearings. Until the late 1880s most machines had plain bearings calling for constant oiling, though by then the hard-to-adjust roller type was being fitted, and ball bearings were available for an extra charge. It sometimes happened that the small back wheel of the penny-farthing seized up entirely as a result of infrequent oiling.

In *The Wheels of Chance*, H. G. Wells introduces a clergyman whose tricycle has become 'no better than a heavy chair without castors'. He attributes this to his man having

> carefully washed out the bearings with paraffin, and let the machine dry without oiling it again. The consequence was that they became heated to a considerable temperature and jammed. Even at the outset the machine ran stiffly as well as noisily, and I, being inclined to ascribe this stiffness to my own lassitude, merely redoubled my exertions. It is my rule of life to do whatever I find to do with all my might . . . Finally the entire apparatus became rigid, and I abandoned the unequal contest.

85   *Foot-rests in use*

Frames. The crude wooden frame of the hobby-horses was superseded at the end of the 1860s—when pedalled velocipedes were being made commercially—by a frame of solid wrought iron. The same construction was employed for the early high-wheelers. The latter's frame, incidentally, was the simplest there has ever been; it was just a graceful backbone with forks at each end for the wheels and a steering head. Hollow frames were adopted after 1877 to reduce weight, though inferior high-wheelers were still being made with solid ones in 1880.

Steel tubes, solid-drawn, in conjunction with wrought iron lugs and brackets, came in for the diamond frames of the first safety bicycles in 1885. The Raleigh Cycle Company made an important advance in 1901 when it introduced the first 'all-steel' bicycle. It was made of thin steel tubes, lugs and brackets stamped from sheet steel and was thus much lighter. Bicycles became lighter still with the invention of the butt-ended tube of Reynolds and Hewitt in 1897; and further weight was saved in the 1930s by the use of stronger steel. Tentative methods of construction, other than the now generally adopted brazed-tube-and-lug method, have included frames made of brazed laminated tube, and even bamboo.

Pedalling mechanisms. The transmission of the rider's effort to the driving wheel, simple enough when the pedals were directly attached to the cranks on the front wheel, was a matter for vigorous experiment during the 1880s. Forms of transmission tried out during this period included the lever, epicyclic gear, independent ratchet, pivoted lever, steel band and both front and rear-driving chains. The final form, the rear chain drive, was satisfactorily developed in 1885 but not generally adopted until ten years later. This arrangement has now been in continuous use for well over half a century and is an inherent feature of the standard diamond-frame safety bicycle.

The rear shaft drive, a more compact variation of this basic arrangement, was used to a small extent during the first few years of the 20th century. It was not popular. A. C. Pemberton, writing in 1897 in *The Complete Cyclist*, said that his experience with shafts and their toothed gears had proved to him that they wasted more power than chains and were prone to develop a nasty vibration for the feet.

He said that, as a practical engineer, he knew only too well the difficulties of cutting bevel gears: they could be made only approximately true by running a cutter through the wheel twice and so averaging the curves. The shafts revolved very easily when lightly loaded and exhibited on a stand in a shop window, but when hard pressed the difference in the way they worked was marked. The friction increased in a greater ratio than the increase in load. At that date the lady's shaft-driven bicycle had no sheath round the revolving shaft, so the rider was always liable to the dangerous chance of getting her skirt wound round it. Pemberton adds this comment:

> I have seen a three-inch shaft take hold of a handkerchief tied round a cut on a workman's hand, and break his arm in many places, his life only being saved by the strap driving it coming off. If this could happen with a large polished shaft, it is easy to understand how a small one revolving among the numerous folds of a lady's skirt might obtain such a hold as to tear it from the rider's back.

Shortly after this was written, all shafts were fitted with protective devices.

The invention of the differential gear had allowed the outer driving wheel of early tricycles to overrun the inner when turning. The free-wheel device, incorporating a ratchet, was invented in 1881; it made mounting and dismounting incomparably easier, and did away with the occasion for foot-rests, but did not become at all usual on bicycles till after the turn of the century. One reason was the uncertainty of most brakes (where any were carried): speed was customarily checked by back-pedalling, though only at the expense of great strain when the machine was going fast.

Richard Church records in *Over the Bridge* that in 1900 his mother bought his father a new bicycle, 'with a modern invention called a "free-wheel"'; it was also equipped with Bowden brakes, a new type acting on the rims and operated by cables. Mr. Church's father had hungered for such a bicycle, tempted by the advertisements in the magazine *Cycling*.

Evidence of widespread use of fixed-pedal bicycles at this time, nearly twenty years after the invention of the free-wheel, is implicit in Pemberton's observations on the foot-rests which gave riders relief from the ever turning pedals.

Foot-rests, he said, were a *sine qua non* for all who wished to tour with ease. Many different patterns were to be obtained. In choosing them, one should see that they were substantial and not calculated to damage the enamel of the forks. Many riders dispensed with their use altogether and made shift with the top of the fork crown. This, in Pemberton's opinion, was a very good substitute, and to be preferred indeed when the crown was broad and flat, as it commonly was. If the top plate were to be lengthened and turned up, said Pemberton, it would become a perfect rest and do away with the weight and unsightliness of the ordinary fork crown which, like the step, often caught and tore at the garments of the rider.

Gears. A gear to make the driving wheel go further, and therefore theoretically faster, was fitted by Starley to his Ariel penny-farthing as early as 1870. It could not be changed. The gearing of the chain driven bicycles, which is dependent on the axle size over which the chain runs, was a topic much discussed by the first riders of these machines.

Men were accustomed to telling enquirers what their gearing was—fifty, say, or sixty—and why a particular size seemed best suited to their physiques. The gearing size could often be quite simply calculated: for example, if the twenty-eight-inch back wheel of the safety went round twice for each stroke of the crank axle, then the machine would be described as geared to fifty-six. Or, in other words, it would be equivalent to pedalling a penny-farthing machine with a wheel of fifty-six inches.

A gearing of sixty-three, they used to say, was about the right size for men who were not particularly athletic and preferred ease to speed. The young man wishing to perform great feats would not be satisfied with less than seventy, and the racing man liked something over a hundred. Ladies, it was thought, were best suited with about fifty-six, though if they were exceptionally strong they could perhaps manage sixty. The point about women's bicycles was that they had shorter cranks which meant less leverage and the need for rather more pressure on the pedals. Riders were told that the only way to find out which gear suited them best was by actual trial. They were asked to remember that while a big gear was perfect with a following wind and a good road, it appeared, when conditions were the reverse, to grow higher and higher every mile until at last the rider was run to a standstill.

The weight of late Victorian bicycles emphasized the need for some means of changing the gear to a lower one while going along. Forms of hub and derailleur speed gears produced in the 1890s were fitted successfully to safety bicycles and were the forerunners of the perfected types which came in soon after 1900. The three-speed hub gear of Sturmey-Archer, 1902, and of Armstrong-Triplex, 1906, established the principles on which such types of speed gear have ever since been made.

Wheels. The heavy wheels of the hobby-horse and the early boneshaker were similar to those of small carts. They had load-bearing spokes of wood or metal and, of course, little resilience. A very different principle was adopted for the lordly driving wheel of the penny-farthing. This was a suspension wheel in that the weight it carried was hung or suspended on fine wire spokes.

There were various methods of building such wheels. In the usual method rolled steel rims of V, U or crescent section were constructed of two separate circles, one having a deeper section than the other; the two circles were brazed together to form one hollow rim within which were the screwed spoke nipples. Single steel rims were also common; some riders insisted on wooden rims.

In the early days of the high-wheeler spokes were of the radial variety, running directly from hub to rim, but in 1874 Starley invented the tangent-spoke wheel in which the spokes are set aslant so that each pair crosses each other at an angle. This arrangement gave great strength and rigidity for low weight and has been in use ever since.

Tyres. The iron tyre had been gratefully abandoned for both boneshakers and penny-farthings by 1871. The solid rubber tyre had a wire running through the centre; various adhesives were used to help it stay firm on the rim. If it came off on a journey it could be tied on again

87   *Air-filled tyres*

with a piece of string or wire. Of the pneumatic tyre introduced in 1889 (and discussed already), this is what Lacy Hillier, writing in 1895, had to say:

> It is difficult to estimate the increase it has made in the average pace of the cycle, whilst it has not only made the task of propulsion at a given pace so much the easier, but has also materially reduced the vibration—a point which specially appeals to the elderly and more nervous rider. The younger cyclists, when the tyre was first introduced, were apparently not conscious of the vibration . . . but without doubt they would be fully aware of it today if they changed from their air-tyred machines to the solid-tyred cycles of 1888.

Brakes. The better boneshakers had back-wheel brakes consisting of either a spoon or a shoe which pressed down on the tyre; it was operated by a cord from the handle bar. A number of the high-wheelers had no brakes at all; riders were expected to provide the braking power by back-pedalling. When brakes were fitted it was nearly always to the front wheel. They were of the spoon type, poised just above the tyre in front of the steering head and operated by a hand lever. They were so effective that incautious application caused a forward somersault. Ground brakes were tried. Since they acted directly on the road they were very powerful; bicycles having them were made with especially stout backbones.

Satisfactory brakes for use with the pneumatic tyre was a lasting problem for the designers of safety bicycles. By the end of the century nearly all makers were beginning to see the importance of fitting brakes, but most of them, according to Pemberton, could not have been better designed if their object was to wear down the tyre by friction rather than to check speed. Brakes still consisted, basically, of iron shoes operating on the top of the front tyre. Heavy employment of them could quickly spoil the new air-filled Dunlop kind. *Punch* published some verses entitled 'To Marie, riding my bicycle', parodying a famous poem by Tennyson:

Brake, brake, brake
  On my brand-new tyre, Marie!
And I would that my tongue could utter
  The thoughts that arise in me.

O well for the fishmonger's boy
  That his tricycle's mean and squalid;
O well for the butcher lad
  That the tyres of his wheel are solid!

And the reckless scorchers scorch
  With hanging purple heads,
But O for the tube that is busted up
  And the tyre that is cut to shreds.

Brake, brake, brake—
  Thou hast broken indeed, Marie,
And the rounded form of my new Dunlop
  Will never come back to me.

Pemberton deplored the fact that the public in general showed little interest in having a brake. The majority of riders, he said, would find a trustworthy brake, if such could be obtained, a great aid to fast travel. The rider, assured that he had a reliable check on his momentum when needed, would be able to coast down unknown hills at a most exhilarating pace. With a brake many an accident could be avoided: accidents caused by children's pleasure in darting unexpectedly into the roads, by carts suddenly deviating from their course. The difficulty of stopping a bicycle by back-pedalling had been increased, he said, by the higher gearing of modern machines. With a big gear

> the rider may actually stand on the pedals without stopping the machine. Some riders, when in difficulties, form an extemporary brake by inserting their toe between the forks of the front wheel, and pressing down the foot on the tyre. This is a very certain and powerful method of pulling up . . . and one which should be remembered should a brake give way.

Pemberton did not, however, recommend this procedure as a substitute for a brake because of the wear to the soles of shoes and because 'the heat generated by friction will prove most unpleasant on a long descent'. In any case, braking with the foot in this way was impossible when mudguards were fitted. (These were unpopular at this period because of their weight and tendency to rattle.)

Something had to be done about brakes when the free-wheel bicycles at last became fashionable: now the rider had no way of slowing down with the pedals. A moderately effective wheel-rim brake for both front and rear wheels was introduced soon after 1900, a type still available today. As the shoe-on-tyre brake was increasingly found wanting, so a whole variety of new designs emerged. These included the caliper rim brake, the contracting band brake, the coaster-hub brake and the internally expanding brake.

Cyclometers. The considerable distances which could be covered by the high-wheeler—and which most riders passionately wished to cover—created a need for the cyclometer by means of which the distance travelled could be automatically recorded. The cyclometer was regarded as a cherished fitting whose absence would have deprived cyclists of an important part of their satisfaction.

The mechanism was mounted either on the hub of the front wheel, when the mileage done was recorded through a tumbler action, or on the forks at the side of the front wheel when it was driven through a cog-wheel or trip mechanism.

One of the most popular of the early types was the Thompson cyclometer, patented by J. C. Thompson in 1877. Inside a cylindrical casing resembling a kitchen alarm clock was a train of gear wheels connected with three indicating dials; the readings were in yards, miles and tens of miles. The maximum reading was a hundred miles. It was necessary, of course, to have the right cyclometer for one's wheel size; thus a Thompson on view at the Science Museum in London is for use with the fifty-inch driving wheel.

Some cyclometers incorporated a bell which rang out at the end of each mile. More compact versions, recording both total mileage and individual journey mileage, were introduced after 1900. In the 1930s came miniature speedometers of the motor-cycle type which showed speed as well as mileage. These gadgets for bicycles are still asked for—by those touring cyclists who brave the main roads of today—and the firms who make them have had to undertake the extra work of providing readings in the metric system.

But it is not within the scope of this book to discuss recent developments in any detail. Indeed they have been few, apart from the coming in the early 1960s of the small-wheeled, cross-framed Moulton; the conventional diamond-framed safety still has pride of place among the cycles to be seen on the roads, as may be confirmed by a visit to Cambridge or to the other places where bicycles are much used. The Edwardian bicycle had some 300 component parts. It still has. When suitably fixed to one another, they offer the cheapest and smallest form of transport—and perhaps a good potential answer to congestion in the streets of London.

Sport

Bicycling and tricycling began as a sport—unlike ski-ing which began as a way of getting about. For many they have always been a sport, a pursuit which is traditionally and correctly known as cycling. There is a great difference between the point of view of the enthusiastic cyclist and that of the bicyclist on his way to work or the shops.

Cycling in an organized form is much less than the rage it was in the early years of the 20th century, but a glance at the cycling press gives evidence enough of the prominent part it still has in national life. In many countries cycling-club activities remain well developed. In the late 1960s indeed, British clubs, scattered over the country, could boast of having more members, collectively, than in the 1950s.

Thousands of teams of riders are to be seen during summer weekends whirring along the country lanes and —less happily—on the big main roads. With little apparent exertion, they may be keeping up a steady 25 to 30 miles an hour. The riders are in pairs; in front is the captain and at the back the second in command, ready to give warning of vehicles about to overtake. It is not uncommon to encounter the solitary hard rider, head down, tearing along at well over 40 miles an hour; he

88   *An early club run*

is probably trying to beat a record over a measured route. One sees, too, the occasional young man in singlet and brief white shorts propelling a lightweight tricycle with surprising speed.

Not all these people are young; many own cars and motor bicycles: cycling is their pleasure, mentally as well as physically. They even enjoy maintenance work on their machines. The really keen club member will wash his chain periodically in a bath of paraffin and then immerse it in hot molten grease in order to lubricate thoroughly the interior of every link.

Cycling clubs began to be formed almost as soon as the bicycle appeared. The organization of them has always been largely social; and the runs they offer are often divided into potterers' and hard riders' sections. The biggest club is the Cyclists' Touring Club (formed in 1878, and several times referred to in these pages), which has members scattered throughout Europe and North America.

Many other countries have national clubs. All make it their business to publish road books, maps and journals. They recommend hotels, with fixed rates, in their own and other countries. They appoint representatives to be of use to members while touring, and have succeeded in inducing most governments to allow cyclists to travel freely across frontiers without paying duty on their machines. In all countries they have put up warning signs at dangerous places.

Cycle racing on track and road had a strictly commercial origin. The manufacturers employed professional riders to ride as fast as they could between two points, thereby, with luck, advertising the superiority of their machines.

Track racing began at the Crystal Palace in 1869 and in ten years had spread to all the big towns. Championship races were established in 1878 at the time of the founding on the National Cyclists' Union and when, incidentally, the sport was recognized by Oxford and Cambridge. In 1882 H. L. Cortis was the first to cycle at over 20 miles an hour—on, of course, a penny-farthing. In 1883 John Keen, then the leading professional cyclist, covered 50 miles in 3 hours 6¾ minutes. A list of such records could be prolonged indefinitely. To those familiar with modern performances the speeds seem very slow until it is remembered that surfaces were almost invariably rough and the tyres—until 1890—solid.

In 1899 Charles M. Murphy made a sensation in America by pedalling a mile in one minute behind a train. A wooden track had been laid between the rails and an elaborate wind shelter built on the back of the train. At the first attempt the locomotive could not reach the required speed and a larger engine was brought up.

M

89 *Track racing, 1875*

During the successful mile-a-minute ride the weight of this engine caused so much rocking of the track that Murphy was shaken out of his shelter. He retrieved his position only by a supreme effort. Then, at the end of the measured mile, he ran into the back of the train as a result of the engine drive shutting off steam too abruptly. However, helpers posted on a rear platform managed to haul him safely aboard. His speed of 60 miles an hour is today reached unaided on favourable stretches of road by riders in the great national cycling tours.

The earliest, and still the most famous of these events, is the Tour de France. It was founded in 1903 by Henri Desgrange (who 10 years earlier had ridden 21 miles in one hour). Some 3000 miles have to be covered in about 25 days.

The Tour de France soon became so spectacular and interesting to the public that other European countries instituted similar tours. There is the Giro d'Italia, for example. There is the Tour of Egypt and the Tour of Tunisia, both of them events which attract the world's leading professional cyclists. Great cycle races are also staged annually in Asia, South America, Canada and Australia. Millions attend them. In the United States the big road races of recent years have been the Tour of Somerville, the Grand Prix of Long Island, the Connecticut Valley Championship and the Eastern Seaboard Championship. According to statistics compiled by cycle manufacturers in the early 1960s, some 27 million Americans then rode bicycles. There has recently been a marked revival of interest in cycling as a sport.

The road race has been divided into two major kinds. In Britain the most usual kind is the time trial in which each rider is timed individually. Instead of setting off together in a bunch, the competitors are released by a starter at minute intervals and follow a course that is marshalled by officials posted at corners and bends. Most of the trials are held at times when there is little traffic, such as early in the morning on Sundays. This class of racing, devised to attract the least public attention and interference with ordinary traffic, began in the 1890s when the police raised objections to racing in line.

Massed start racing, as practised on the Continent, can be more exciting for the riders and is certainly more attractive for those watching; but because of the supposed danger involved on British roads, few such races were organized in the first fifty years of the 20th century. Both the National Cyclists' Union and the Road Time Trials Council (formed in 1922) were against massed start racing. They had become convinced that any ordinary form of racing on the public roads would be condemned by the Ministry of Transport and the Home Office, and that attempts to introduce such racing would provoke restrictive legislation which would adversely affect other forms of competitive cycling.

The fact that massed start racing now does take place in Britain is the result of the efforts of the British League of Racing Cyclists, formed during the Second World War. The sponsors of this body refused to accept the belief, widely held for half a century, that racing on British roads was of doubtful legality. In spite of forbidding statements about the official attitude from the Ministry of Transport, the B.L.R.C. proceeded, with the support of manufacturers and various newspapers, to organize a series of massed start races. The N.C.U. was greatly annoyed, seeing all kinds of trouble ahead.

However, the B.L.R.C. went on to arrange, in 1951, a tour of Britain on the lines of the famous Tour de France. This was followed by none of the dire consequences vaguely threatened by the Ministry of Transport. In fact it was shown that the British public warmed to cycle racing and that, so long as they were carefully organized in collaboration with the police, road events of the Continental kind could be held in Britain with advantage to cycling sport and industry. Certain legal restrictions issued in 1960 set out rules for the timing and location of the races. No extra restriction was imposed on the traditional procedure for conducting time trials.

The industry

It is believed that nearly ten million bicycles, widely differing in age, are today in use from time to time in Britain, an average of one for every five inhabitants (in Holland the corresponding figure is one between four people and in Denmark one between two). Most of Britain's existing bicycles were made by Raleigh Industries, or by firms like Rudge-Whitworth, Phillips or Hercules which have become part of the Raleigh empire. Even when the manufacture of components and accessories is included, Raleigh are found to control about three-quarters of Britain's cycle industry; more than three-quarters of what they make is exported to 140 countries.

In the last years of the nineteenth century there were dozens of fair-sized cycle firms: several have been referred to in this book. There were also scores of small traders making up machines for local sale, often to order, from standard parts supplied to them by established manufacturers. Bespoke customers tended to be particular about which manufacturer's parts should go into their bicycle or tricycle. B.S.A., in their catalogue for the trade of 1899, refer to 'numerous complaints from purchasers of machines' who had ordered B.S.A. fittings

90   *Raleigh's Carlton Clubman, with five-speed derailer gear, 1969*

and been supplied with either imitations or incomplete sets:

> The company wishes it to be clearly understood that
> what is known as a B.S.A. set consists of nine parts,
> viz., 1 Bottom Bracket, 1 Ball Head, 2 Fork Ends
> with Parallel Chain Adjustment, 1 seat Lug, 2 Hubs,
> and 2 Pedals.

The slump at the end of the 1890s put a number of bicycle firms out of business or drove them to make other things—those who could afford the plant turned to the motor-car field. Since around 1900, the number of cycle firms, large and small, has steadily diminished, Raleigh alone expanding and remaining in good order. A sketch, at least, of the development of Raleigh Industries Ltd. seems appropriate here.

The building up of the business was the work of Frank Bowden, once a household name for his Bowden rim-acting brake; he was eventually knighted. In 1877 he retired, a sick man, from business in Hong Kong and came home with 'only a few months to live'. On the advice of a Harrogate doctor, Bowden took up bicycling.

91   *Moulton, 1967*

Within six months he found himself perfectly fit again and so much impressed by the potentialities of the bicycle that he sought out the makers of the machine he had been riding. In Raleigh Street, Nottingham, he was directed to the firm of Woodhead and Angois and entered a small workshop where twelve men were turning out three penny-farthings a week.

Bowden proceeded to acquire an interest in the concern and then formed the Raleigh Cycle Company, financed and controlled by himself. Already a successful businessman, he did the controlling to such effect that by 1896—in less than ten years—Raleigh had the largest cycle works in Britain. It occupied seven and a half acres and employed 850 people.

At that time annual production of machines was around 30,000. And there is no doubt that all were made as strongly as possible, that the company's well-publicized policy of 'quality before quantity' was no idle boast. A woman who bought a Raleigh bicycle in 1898 wrote to the firm twenty years later to tell them that 'never once in that time has any repair been done . . . it runs today like a new machine'.

In its advertising Raleigh concentrated on the health

aspects of bicycling. In the early 1920s, when it was clear that the bicycle, as well as the tricycle, had lost some of its appeal to the motor-car, Raleigh went all out to make customers of factory workers, clerks and shop assistants. It was worth saving up, said Raleigh, to buy the means of enjoying 'a refreshing weekly ride in the open air'. To ride a Raleigh, in fact, made life worth living.

A glossy Raleigh pamphlet of 1923 begins with the words: 'Is your life spent among whirring machinery, in adding up columns of figures, in attending to the wants of often fractious customers?' Sketches of beauty spots and historic buildings surround on each page the various bicycle models on offer. The opening text continues:

Don't you sometimes long to get away from it all? Away from the streets of serried houses . . . only a few miles away is a different land, where the white road runs between the bluebell-covered banks crowned by hedges from which the pink and white wild rose peeps a shy welcome.

Sheltering amongst the trees you see the spire of the village church—beyond it that quaint old thatched cottage where the good wife serves fresh eggs and ham fried 'to a turn' on a table of rural spotlessness, for everything is so *clean* in the country. . . .

Rosy health and a clear brain is what Raleigh gives you. . . .

In 1933 Raleigh made 200,000 machines; they had taken over production of Humber cycles. In 1943 they took over the Rudge-Whitworth Cycle Company and between 1952 and 1957 acquired the interests of B.S.A. and Triumph. The rest of the industry was largely controlled at this stage by the British Cycle Corporation which was responsible for the range of machines labelled Phillips, Hercules, Sun, Armstrong and Norman. In 1960, this group, a subsidiary of Tube Investments, was merged with Raleigh Industries. Raleigh, it was arranged, should be the cycle division of Tube Investments.

The cause of all these mergers in the 1950s was increased affluence before which the bicycle—surely just a workman's machine?—was fast losing ground. Sales in Britain fell by half between 1950 and 1960. Abroad, low-priced machines made in Japan, and elsewhere in the Far East, closed several traditional markets.

In the late 1950s, however, Alex Moulton of Bradford-on-Avon was developing the first entirely new design for a bicycle in over half a century: his bicycle was to halt the trend towards steadily diminishing sales.

The Moulton had sixteen-inch wheels, slimly tyred, and an open frame reminiscent of the long-abandoned cross frame. Like the safety of the 1880s, this tiny-wheeled machine seemed at first a sort of joke, or at best a young person's plaything; but the briefest trial revealed an underestimate. It would not only go as fast as an ordinary bicycle—the gearing saw to that—but it would do this with ease, so lively was the response to the pedals brought about by a low centre of gravity. As for road bumps, all but the worst were dealt with by a new kind of rubber suspension device fore and aft (in the early days Mr. Moulton used to demonstrate prototypes on a badly pot-holed drive at his house).

In 1959 Mr. Moulton offered his design to Raleigh Industries. They rejected it; the public, they said, would never take to so unusual a machine. Mr. Moulton decided to go ahead on his own and began making Moulton bicycles at Bradford-on-Avon.

To Raleigh's surprise and embarrassment, he did remarkably well. The Moulton became fashionable, even glamorous; it was bought by people who had come to associate all bicycles with the proletarian cloth cap. It won several important awards. In 1962 John Woodburn of Reading, riding a Moulton, improved on the Cardiff-to-London record by 18 minutes; he rode 162 miles in 6 hours 44 minutes. No one who saw him darting through the heavy traffic between Northolt and Marble Arch at nearly 30 miles an hour could doubt that this was a man's machine.

Raleigh Industries were becoming almost flustered. In the summer of 1965 they launched a small-wheeled

92   *Raleigh's Twenty, recommended 'for house-weary wives', 1969*

bicycle of their own, the RSW 16 (Raleigh Small-Wheel 16 inch). By that time sales of Moulton bicycles had reached 70,000.

Unable to use Mr. Moulton's suspension system, Raleigh fitted instead exceptionally fat tyres. These did have the effect of softening road jolts, but they also made the bicycles relatively sluggish in performance.

In 1967, following twelve months in which their turnover and profits had gone down eight per cent., Raleigh did a deal with Mr. Moulton, buying his concern and at the same time retaining his services as consultant. They admitted they had been wrong nine years earlier to reject Mr. Moulton's designs; Leslie Roberts, then chairman of Raleigh, told the newspapers that he blamed 'bad market research'.

There is at present no reason to think that small-wheelers will completely oust the conventional bicycle with 26-inch wheels, which is still preferred by racing men. Some people just dislike the look of them; others object to being unable to ride without hands and to the fact that no excellence of suspension will persuade the little wheels to bowl over an obstacle like a curbstone. Nevertheless Raleigh could report at the end of the

1960s that Moulton-type bicycles (with a choice of 20- and 16-inch wheels) accounted for thirty per cent of their total sales in Britain.

Recent developments have had to do with modifications of Mr. Moulton's original suspension system. This has been strengthened and improved to a point at which it is possible to question the continued need for air-filled, and still puncture-prone, tyres. At the time of writing Mr. Moulton is experimenting with the kind of solid rubber tyre in use in the 1880s.

Index